HeartSmart™ Chinese Cooking

Stephen Wong

**HEART
AND STROKE
FOUNDATION
OF CANADA**

Douglas & McIntyre
1615 Venables Street
Vancouver, British Columbia
V5L 2H1

Canadian Cataloguing in Publication Data

Wong, Stephen, 1955–
HeartSmart Chinese cooking

Includes index.
ISBN 1-55054-496-6

1. Cookery, Chinese. 2. Low-fat diet—Recipes. I. Heart and Stroke Foundation of Canada. II. Title. III. Title: Heart smart Chinese cooking.
TX724.5.C5W66 1996   641.5'638   C96-910239-9

Editing by Elizabeth Wilson
Cover and text design by DesignGeist
Photography by John Sherlock
Photography assistance by Mark Gilbert
Illustrations by Rose Cowles
Printed and bound in Canada by Friesens

Contents

Acknowledgements

We would like to thank the following team who contributed their professional experience, insight, dedication and humour to this cookbook:
HSF, Canada—Bill Tholl, Executive Director; Doug MacQuarrie, Director, Health Promotion.
HSF, B.C. & Yukon—Richard Rees, Executive Director; Fiona Ahrens, Director, Marketing and Communications; Ursula Fradera, M.Sc., Registered Dietitian; Leanne Johnson, B.A.; Brenda Hewer; George Ng, D.D.S.; Boon Wong, M.D.
HSF, Ontario—Rick Gallop, Executive Director; Carol Dombrow, B.Sc., Registered Dietitian; Ernest Ng, C.A., Chinese Canadian Council.

Sincere thanks to:
James Kennedy, DMATP, and his team of chef training students; the Board of Directors of the B.C. & Yukon Foundation for supporting the development of this book; Scott McIntyre and his team for their enthusiasm in bringing the book to market; Stephen Wong, visionary and chef.

The Heart and Stroke Foundation

My sincere thanks go to Nancy Ling for her expert and insightful guidance on the nutritional aspects of this book, her meticulous efforts in the recipe testing process and her generosity with her time. I am greatly indebted to James Kennedy for his vast culinary knowledge and flawless technique and his willingness to share secrets and recipes. I owe my words to the best editor, Elizabeth Wilson, who taught me to write shorter and better and patiently kept me on track. I thank Ursula Fradera for her support and confidence in me and Fiona Ahrens for her wealth of ideas and impeccable judgement on the direction of the book.

Above all, I thank my family for their love, faith and encouragement. I also thank all the people in the local food industry who have helped me to be who I can be.

Stephen Wong

James Kennedy oversaw the testing and helped develop the recipes for this book. He is a pioneer in HeartSmart cooking, with fifteen years of experience in lower-fat, lower-sodium recipe development. As owner-operator of NV Food & Service Resource Group Ltd., he is a respected name in cook training and curriculum development in B.C.

Nancy Ling, Registered Dietitian, tested and analyzed all the recipes in this book and wrote the introduction "Healthy Eating the Chinese Way." In her work she provides nutrition education and rehabilitation to homebound patients and people with heart disease.

Preface

For over forty years the Heart and Stroke Foundation has been the champion of heart research and health promotion in the interest of reducing the burden of heart disease and stroke for all Canadians.

Findings from that research and the overall reduction by nearly 50% in the death rate from heart and blood-vessel disease show that simple, everyday lifestyle changes CAN make a difference to your health.

Currently our library of HeartSmart™ cookbooks includes three winners:

- *The Lighthearted Cookbook*
- *Lighthearted Everyday Cooking*
- *Simply HeartSmart Cooking*

They are all aimed at making daily cooking a joyful, creative, flavour-filled experience with the added security of knowing that you are producing healthy meals. We are proud to present *HeartSmart Chinese Cooking*, a delicious journey into the exotic and enticing flavours of China.

Our chef, Stephen Wong, has assembled an array of recipes that proves you don't have to compromise on flavour when cooking Chinese food the HeartSmart way.

Registered dietitian Nancy Ling has included guidelines for healthy eating, the sidebars offer techniques and tips, and the whole book is filled with intriguing folklore.

I believe that you will find *HeartSmart Chinese Cooking* to be both entertaining and informative. I hope you will find a daily adventure in nutritious food!

Gary Sutherland

Gary Sutherland
President, Heart and Stroke Foundation of Canada

The chop, or Chinese stamp, used as a design element throughout the book is a stylized representation of the phrase "long life," which is our hope for everyone.

Introduction

Welcome to my kitchen.

As a new immigrant during the mid-seventies, I was surprised and delighted to discover that Chinese food was already as much a part of Canadian life as hockey. My cooking career began in a French bistro, and before long I began exploring the possibilities of combining western and eastern cooking. What later came to be known as Pacific Rim cooking has been my consuming passion for almost two decades.

In this book I've included some dishes that go back hundreds of years, some that remind me of my Hong Kong childhood and others that combine the multi-ethnic influences that surround me in Vancouver.

Together, while revisiting some simple, familiar techniques, we'll create new dishes that are flavourful, colourful and above all, healthful. We've also discovered some new HeartSmart ways of cooking old standbys—with stocks that boost flavour while replacing oil, and seasonings and condiments that help reduce the need for salt.

We'll make it easy to add variety, that all-important spice, by inviting you to explore a new world of food in the Asian markets and ethnic aisles in your supermarket. Discover gai lan and chayotes, see qua and yard-long beans. Crunch wood ear mushrooms and lotus roots; add zip to your beef with satay sauce; sweeten your chicken with fresh mangoes and discover that tofu doesn't have to taste bland after all. While we're introducing you to Chinese ingredients that you might have been passing by before, we'll also suggest substitutes so you can take advantage of what's available seasonally and regionally.

Some lists of ingredients may seem long, but most recipes feature sauces and marinades which involve simply measuring and stirring. And if some of the instructions seem involved, don't worry—they're mostly directions on how to cut, prepare and mix ingredients before you start cooking. Once you're ready, the cooking time is usually as short as five to ten minutes.

I hope you'll make these recipes your own and use them as the basis to create your own favourites.

Stephen Wong, 1996

Healthy Eating the Chinese Way

Explore a new world of flavours, textures and ingredients—prepared the HeartSmart way.

In traditional Chinese cooking the basic ingredients contain small to moderate amounts of fat. Most fat and sodium is added during preparation to enhance flavour. Our challenge has been to offer you dishes rich in taste and texture and lower in fat and salt. In this book we've combined the most up-to-date ideas about nutrition with the flavours of an ancient cuisine.

Vegetables—A Rainbow of Variety

Chinese cooking makes abundant use of vegetables. Stir-frying preserves their crunchy texture, vivid colour, delicate flavour and vitamin content. The leafy green vegetables and squashes in these dishes are loaded with the antioxidant vitamins C, E and beta carotene, which are currently being researched for their ability to protect against cardiovascular disease and cancer; in particular, vitamin E may play a role in reducing the risk of artery blockage. Dark green leafy vegetables are also a good source of calcium. Try Gai Lan with Oyster Sauce (p. 112), Sauteed Mustard Greens with Garlic (p. 113), or Sauteed Pea Sprouts and Oyster Mushrooms (p. 120) the next time you're looking for calcium-rich vegetable dishes.

Fill Your Plate with Grains

Our recipes are not only lower in fat and sodium, they're a great source of fibre from vegetables and complex carbohydrates. Rice or noodles are an important part of any Chinese meal. *Canada's Food Guide To Healthy Eating* recommends 5 to 12 servings of grain products a day. Steamed Rice (p. 28) or Gingered Brown Rice (p. 29) can go along with any dish from this book for a satisfying, healthy meal. Peppered Beef with Shanghai Noodles (p. 32) or Spinach Fettuccine with Moo Shu Prawns (p. 33) are centrepieces when served with a vegetable dish.

Top Off Your Plate with Meats and Alternatives

In traditional Chinese cooking, meat complements a dish rather than being the focus of the meal. When your plate is filled with vegetables and rice or noodles, plus a flavourful dish like Spicy Beef with Baby Bok Choy (pp. 86-87) or Braised Pork Tenderloin with Chayote (p. 84), you won't notice the reduced amount of meat.

Antioxidants

Research shows that blood cholesterol is more likely to settle along the artery walls when it reacts with an unstable form of oxygen. Antioxidants may neutralize this highly reactive oxygen before it can react with cholesterol, thus preventing atherosclerosis.

Meat alternatives are popular in Chinese dishes and tofu is tops! It can contribute significant amounts of calcium to your diet. The texture of tofu varies from soft and custardlike to firm (which has had the water pressed out). Recipes like our Potsticker Tofu with Shrimp (p. 106), Mushroom Tofu Stir-fry (p. 104), and Baked Tofu Rolls (p. 102) are simple and tasty sources of protein, calcium, and other nutrients.

How Much Fat is Too Much?

The average Canadian adult consumes too much fat (38% of daily calories). Although fat is an important part of a healthy diet (as a source of essential fatty acids and fat-soluble vitamins), this overconsumption partly explains why heart disease, cancer and obesity are so prevalent. Canada's Nutrition Recommendations advise Canadians to cut back their fat intake to 30% of their daily calories (see box).

Fat Cutting Secrets

The challenge for Chef Stephen Wong was to create full flavours and mouthwatering appeal using little fat. Here are some of his secrets:

Substitute high-fat ingredients with lower-fat ones
We have simply replaced oil in many of our recipes with thickened stocks, those old fashioned, easy-to-prepare basics! When moderating the amount of fat in a dish, it is essential to add plenty of flavour and use plenty of liquid to disperse it. We did this by using stocks as the basis for our sauces and thickening them with cornstarch. See the simple stock recipes on pages 2 to 8.

Here are some other amazing substitutions. Try our Sui Choy with Cream Sauce (p. 118), where heavy cream is substituted with skim milk powder. In Baked Twin Lobster in Coconut Curry (p. 68), skimmed coconut milk is the base for a flavourful sauce. Our Fresh Mango Pudding (p. 129) is prepared with 2% evaporated milk instead of light (10%) cream; the fat savings are substantial, and you won't lose on taste.

Most noodles are a good source of low-fat carbohydrates, but they may come with hidden fat: for example, packaged instant noodles are deep-fried during processing, and freshly made noodles, sold in specialty stores, are often tossed in oil before packaging to prevent sticking. Look for the uncooked varieties.

Use a good non-stick pan or wok
A non-stick pan or wok makes life easier when it's time to wash up, and it enables you to cut down on fat. Use oil sparingly and add a little water if items start to stick to the bottom of the pan.

Tip
Cook noodles in boiling water without oil, then rinse in cold water to prevent sticking. There's no need to toss them in oil.

In our nutritional analyses we provide the grams of fat per serving in each recipe. Use the guidelines below to calculate how many grams of fat make up 30% of your daily intake.

Average woman (requiring 1800–2100 kcal/day): about 65 grams or less

Average man (requiring 2300–3000 kcal/day): about 90 grams or less

Use lower-fat cooking methods

Baking, roasting and broiling are very rare in Chinese cooking, but we've introduced these western cooking methods to oriental dishes to reduce the fat content. Try the Pan-roasted Snapper Fillets with Chinese Ratatouille (p. 54) and the Baked Chicken Chow Mein (p. 46). Traditional Chinese steaming also cuts fat in recipes such as Steamed Chicken Dumplings (p. 34).

Trim fat from meat and poultry

Buy leaner cuts of meat, trim off all visible fat, remove the skin from poultry and prepare smaller servings of meat, fish and poultry (3 ounces or 90 grams per person). The recipes in our cookbook use lean cuts of meat like pork tenderloin and trimmed sirloin. Most of our poultry recipes specify skinless poultry, but often the skin can be left on during cooking and removed before serving, as in Pan-roasted Duck (p. 81), with no effect on the fat content.

Flavour with flair

Fat carries flavour and disperses it throughout a dish. To get the same intensity of taste without the aid of fat you'll need to increase your salt-free seasonings such as garlic, ginger, shallots and cilantro. Combine them with rich-tasting stocks and you're adding flavour the HeartSmart way.

Marinades add flavour and help fish, meat and poultry retain their moisture in cooking, which is important when you're using little fat.

Can Lower-salt Chinese Cooking Taste Good?

Many foods naturally contain sodium, but most sodium is added to foods in the form of salt. Most Canadians consume more sodium than their bodies need—average consumption is around 4 grams per day or more, and a lower-salt diet allows for 2 grams of sodium per day (approximately 1 teaspoonful of salt). Excessive sodium intake can result in fluid retention in susceptible people. Excess fluid makes the heart work harder to pump blood throughout the body, and this can lead to high blood pressure.

These recipes do use sodium-rich sauces, but in limited amounts. Following lower-sodium guidelines, our dishes contain approximately 25% of the sodium content that you would find in a similar restaurant dish. None of our recipes have more than 0.9 grams of sodium per generous serving. Here's how Stephen Wong cut salt without compromising flavour:

Use stocks for flavour

Our cookbook has recipes for six delicious homemade stocks (pp. 2-8), all of which are salt and fat free, unlike commercial stock or bouillon

Remember
1 teaspoon of any fat— margarine, vegetable oil, lard or butter—contains 5 grams of fat!

The HeartSmart criteria for our recipes are based on these guidelines:

Breakfast and morning snack: 10–15 grams fat

Lunch and afternoon snack: 25–35 grams fat

Dinner and evening snack: 25–40 grams fat

cubes. To make your use of these wonderful stocks an everyday event, you can prepare a whole batch ahead of time and freeze it in ice-cube tray portions which you can easily thaw and use later.

Spice it up

To maintain a flavour adventure, the quantity of garlic, ginger, vinegar and other spices is sometimes doubled in our recipes (compared to similar high-fat, high-salt recipes). You can play with salt-free spices like Five-spice Powder, Curry Powder and Vietnamese-style Chili Sauce (pp. 9-10) in your favourite dishes.

Cholesterol Concerns

There are two types of cholesterol: blood cholesterol and dietary cholesterol. Blood cholesterol, which naturally occurs in the body, is a white, waxy substance, manufactured mainly by the liver. We need cholesterol for our bodies to function properly; however, problems can arise if the level of cholesterol in our blood is too high and begins building up on our artery walls.

Of blood cholesterol, there are two types: high-density (HDL) and low-density (LDL). HDL-cholesterol is often referred to as the "good" cholesterol, since it gathers up excess cholesterol in the bloodstream and carries it back to the liver to be excreted. The level of HDL in your blood is mainly influenced by exercise, weight, smoking and genetics.

LDL-cholesterol is often referred to as the "bad" cholesterol because excess levels build up on our artery walls. The fat portion of your diet can play an important role in controlling LDL levels. Foods high in fat, especially saturated fat, may increase LDL-cholesterol levels. It is desirable to have low LDL and high HDL-cholesterol levels.

Cholesterol misconception

Dietary cholesterol is found only in foods of animal origin, primarily egg yolks, shrimp, prawns, liver and, to some extent, dairy products and meat. Many people believe that the cholesterol in foods is mainly responsible for raising their blood cholesterol. You may wonder why so many tempting shellfish and egg recipes appear in our collection: Stir-fried Mussels (p. 61), Spicy Garlic Prawns (p. 62), Steamed Oysters with Garlic Topping (p. 60) and Chinese Fish Frittata (p. 56).

We now know that dietary cholesterol doesn't affect blood cholesterol nearly as much as dietary fat. Moderation is the key. High-cholesterol foods can be eaten a few times a week but should not be part of your daily diet.

If you're concerned about your blood cholesterol level, pay more attention to the total fat content in your diet, and particularly saturated fat, than to dietary cholesterol. When you cut back on fat, you automatically reduce your cholesterol intake!

High Cholesterol

If you are diagnosed with a blood cholesterol problem, you may be advised to restrict consumption of high-cholesterol foods. These foods may have some effect on the blood cholesterol of sensitive individuals.

Fat Facts

Saturated fat

Saturated fats tend to raise LDL-cholesterol levels. The main food sources are meat, poultry, dairy products, butter, lard and tropical oils (palm and coconut oil).

Since the Chinese diet traditionally uses few dairy products, less saturated fat comes from this food group. However, some Chinese dishes include fatty meats and poultry. We have modified conventional recipes such as Chiu Chow Lemon Duck Soup (p. 72), Pan-roasted Duck (p. 81) and Barbecued Pork (p. 97) by removing the skin from poultry or choosing leaner cuts of meat.

Monounsaturated fat

This type of fat seems to lower "bad" LDL-cholesterol levels and may also increase the "good" HDL-cholesterol. Monounsaturated fats are primarily found in olive and canola oils, soft margarines made from these oils, and hazelnuts, almonds, pistachios, pecans and cashews.

Canola oil is used in most of our recipes for several reasons, other than its high monounsaturated fat content: it has the least saturated fat of all fats, it naturally contains small amounts of omega-3 fatty acids and the antioxidant vitamin E, it is inexpensive and it is Canadian produced.

Since nuts are high in fat, we have reduced the amount of nuts from the original recipes by half. This way the fat content is lower, but you can still enjoy the nutritional benefits of nuts. Try Prawns with Cashews and See Qua (p. 64) or Stir-fried Chicken with Mango (p. 76), which features Candied Pecans with Sesame (p. 12).

Polyunsaturated fat

Polyunsaturated fats help lower the "bad" LDL-cholesterol levels in your blood. This type of fat also contains essential fatty acids, which are mainly found in vegetable oils such as safflower, sunflower, corn, soybean, sesame seed and most nut oils, soft margarines made with these oils, walnuts, chestnuts, Brazil and pine nuts, and sesame and sunflower seeds. We have combined nuts with other ingredients in stir-fries to add flavour and texture. See our recipes for Pan-fried Scallops with Pine Nuts (p. 67) or Sesame Spinach (p. 115).

Fish oils or omega-3 fatty acids

Omega-3 fatty acids are a type of polyunsaturated fat found mainly in fatty fish, such as salmon, mackerel, trout and herring. These fish oils promote heart health by reducing the stickiness or clotting tendency of blood. There is strong evidence that fish oils play a role in preventing the formation of blood clots. Fish adds variety to your diet and may lower your risk for heart disease. Enjoy our delicious Salmon Roulades with Enoki Mushrooms (p. 48), Salmon with Szechuan Pepper (p. 49) or Tea-smoked Seafood (p. 63).

Trans fat

Some trans fatty acids occur naturally in foods and others are formed by a chemical process called hydrogenation, which turns liquid vegetable oils solid. Even though trans fatty acids are unsaturated, they seem to have a blood cholesterol-raising capacity similar to saturated fat.

The main source of trans fatty acids is vegetable shortening and processed foods made with it, such as cookies, crackers, snack foods, deep-fried foods, some peanut butters and many (not all) margarines.

Shortening or lard is typically used in Chinese pastries like steamed buns and tart shells. We substituted shortening with vegetable oil in our recipes. The delicious sweet pastry crust we use in Mini Custard Tarts (p. 131) is made with ricotta cheese, flour and a small quantity of butter. These tarts are just as satisfying as commercially prepared ones, but with less fat.

Nancy Ling, Registered Dietitian

Moderation

Knowing that "good" vegetable oils such as canola and olive oil are excellent vehicles for lowering cholesterol levels, some consumers may use large amounts of them. Even though these oils are low in saturated fats, it is the *total* amount of fat in your diet that has the biggest effect on your blood cholesterol level. The moral is— lower all the fat in your diet!

Nutrient Analysis

Nutrient analysis of the recipes was performed by Nancy Ling, Registered Dietitian, using the Food Processor Nutrition Analysis Software, Version 6.03 (ESHA Research, 1995) software program. The nutrient database was the 1991 Canadian Nutrient File supplemented when necessary with documented data from reliable sources.

The analysis was based on:

— imperial weights and measures
— first ingredient listed when there was a choice of ingredients.

Canola oil and homemade unsalted stocks were used throughout.

Specific measures of salt were included in the analyses, but "salt to taste" was not. Use the least salt, soy sauce, etc. that you find acceptable.

Optional ingredients and garnishes in un-specified amounts were not calculated.

Nutrient Information on Recipes

Nutrient values have been rounded to the nearest whole number. Non-zero values less than 0.5 are shown as "trace" (tr).

Steamed rice accompaniment was not included in the recipe analysis.

Good and excellent sources of vitamins (A, C, E, B6, B12, thiamine, niacin, riboflavin, folacin) and minerals (calcium, iron and zinc) have been identified according to the criteria established for nutrition labelling. (Guide for Food Manufacturers and Advertisers, 1988).

A serving that supplies 15% of the Recommended Daily Intake (RDI) for a vitamin or mineral (30% for vitamin C) is a good source of a nutrient. An excellent source must supply 25% of the RDI (50% for vitamin C).

Stocks—The Secret to HeartSmart Chinese Cooking

Stock Tip #1

For convenience, make large batches and freeze the stock in ice-cube trays for easy portioning and storage. Each cube will measure about 1 tablespoon. After the stock is frozen, transfer cubes to freezer bags and label them, then simply take out what you need when you need it.

Stock Tip #2

Save vegetable trimmings, prawn shells, meat and poultry bones and freeze them until you're ready to make stock.

These recipes will help you get the most out of this book. A flavourful stock in cooking is like a good bass in music; it sets the tempo and enriches the tone—it is a seasoning in itself. In HeartSmart Chinese cooking, a stock does even more: it enhances the flavours of the ingredients and so reduces the need for excess salt.

You can buy stocks, but most ready-made ones are high in salt. There are stores and caterers that sell "homemade" stocks, but they don't come cheap.

Making your own stock has so many advantages and takes so little effort. You'll not only have total control over the salt and fat content (none!), you'll also be using up what you might otherwise throw out.

To make your meat or chicken stock completely fat free, refrigerate it after straining. The fat should become a solidified layer at the top, which can easily be removed.

Quick Thickened Stock

This one-step method will turn a thin stock into a lightly thickened stock that works as a replacement for oil. Use it to "fry" noodles or cook vegetables. It will give the food a light oily sheen and provide the moisture to facilitate cooking. This won't freeze, so make as much as you'll need for any recipe that calls for it. The recipe can be multiplied up to four times. (Thick stocks like Veal Demi-glace (p. 7) don't require thickening.)

1¼ cups	chicken or vegetable stock	300 mL
1 tsp	cornstarch	5 mL

Combine stock and cornstarch and mix well. Bring to boil while stirring occasionally. Stock will thicken into a light, oily consistency. Set aside for use.

Yields about 1 cup

Chicken Stock

This is the basic stock of this book. It will work in every recipe that calls for stock. To make it even richer, use 2 lb/1 kg of chicken wings or feet plus 3 lb/1.5 kg of chicken backs and necks.

5 lb	chicken backs and necks, chopped in chunks	2.5 kg
20 cups	cold water	5 L
1	onion, quartered	1
2	cloves garlic, whole	2
1	carrot, chopped	1
1	large leek, trimmed, sliced and cleaned	1
2-inch	piece ginger, thinly sliced	5 cm
1 tsp	Szechuan peppercorns	5 mL
1 tsp	black peppercorns	5 mL

1. Rinse chicken bones thoroughly under cold running water. Drain. Add to large pot with cold water.
2. Over medium heat, bring mixture to slow boil, skimming off foam periodically. When stock starts to boil, add about 1 cup/250 mL cold water to retard boiling. Lower heat and keep pot at steady simmer for about 10 minutes. Continue skimming until surface is mostly clear.
3. Add all vegetables and peppercorns and reduce heat to slow simmer; continue cooking uncovered for about 4 hours. Do not stir and do not allow to boil. Skim surface a few times if necessary.
4. Strain finished stock through strainer lined with double layer of damp cheesecloth to catch solids and much of the fat. Refrigerate and skim off any fat.

Yields about 15 cups/3.75 L

Brown Stock

To make a rich brown stock for use in meat dishes, roast chicken bones in 450°F/230°C oven for 1 hour or until bones are well browned. Cook stock according to recipe and strain through fine-mesh strainer. After straining, return stock to boil and cook until volume is reduced by half.

Vegetable Stock

You can replace any meat or chicken stocks in our recipes with this. A regular vegetable stock calls for a bouquet garni with thyme, bay leaf and parsley. Here we use ginger and lemon grass, so the stock works beautifully in Chinese cooking.

For fuller flavour, different vegetable trimmings such as stems from Chinese mushrooms or watercress can be added during the last 20 minutes of cooking. Waste not, want not.

1 cup	medium onions, chopped	250 mL
1 cup	turnips, chopped	250 mL
2 cups	carrots, chopped	500 mL
2 cups	celery, sliced	500 mL
2 cups	leeks, trimmed, sliced and rinsed	500 mL
1	stalk lemon grass, smashed, chopped	1
2-inch	piece ginger, sliced	5 cm
16 cups	water	4 L

1. In large pot, combine all ingredients and bring to boil. Skim off any foam.
2. Reduce heat to medium and cook uncovered for 45 minutes.
3. Strain stock through fine-mesh sieve or strainer lined with damp cheesecloth. Freeze or refrigerate stock for use in vegetable dishes and soups.

Yields about 15 cups/3.75 L

Chinese-style Vegetable Stock

I prefer soybean sprouts with their yellow beans still attached for this stock because they have a fuller flavour than the more common mung bean sprouts. This is a good stock for stir-fried and braised vegetables.

1 tbsp	vegetable oil	15 mL
3	slices ginger	3
2 lb	soybean sprouts, rinsed and dried	1 kg
¼ cup	dry sherry	50 mL
10	Chinese red dates or 5 dried figs	10
2	stalks Chinese celery or regular celery with leaves, sliced	2
12	Chinese mushroom stems	12
1	large carrot, sliced	1
16 cups	water	4 L

1. Heat oil in stockpot over high heat. Add ginger and saute until fragrant, about 30 seconds. Add bean sprouts and stir for 1 minute.
2. Add sherry, water and rest of ingredients and bring to boil. Reduce heat to medium and cook uncovered for 30 minutes. Skim off oil occasionally.
3. Strain stock through fine-mesh sieve or strainer lined with damp cheesecloth. Freeze or refrigerate stock for use in vegetable dishes and soups.

Yields about 15 cups/3.75 L

Shrimp Stock

Add rich flavour and colour to seafood dishes with this stock. Try to use whole prawns in the shell in your cooking, as they are generally of better quality. After you peel them, reserve the shells and heads. Freeze and accumulate shells until you have time to make this stock. For a more concentrated stock, boil and reduce volume by half after last step.

1 lb	prawn heads and shells	500 g
1 tbsp	oil	15 mL
1	onion, chopped	1
½ cup	carrots, chopped	125 mL
1 cup	leeks, chopped	250 mL
2 tbsp	dried shrimp, optional	25 mL
3	slices ginger	3
2 tbsp	tomato paste	25 mL
1 cup	white wine	250 mL
16 cups	water	4 L

1. Roast prawn shells and heads in 400°F/200°C oven for 20 minutes or until shells are brown.
2. In large saucepan, heat oil and saute onions, carrots, leeks, dried shrimp, ginger and tomato paste for 2 minutes. Add prawn shells and white wine and simmer for 5 minutes. Add water, bring to boil. Skim off any oil and foam. Reduce heat to medium and simmer uncovered for 30 minutes. Skim surface often.
3. Drain stock through fine-mesh strainer. Freeze or refrigerate.

Yields about 14 cups/3.5 L

Veal Demi-glace

This rich stock comes from classical French cooking. It enriches the flavours of practically any beef or red–meat dish.

8 lb	veal bones	4 kg
1 cup	diced onion	250 mL
¾ cup	diced carrot	175 mL
1 cup	diced celery	250 mL
1 cup	tomato paste	250 mL
24 cups	water	6 L

Bouquet Garni:

1	bay leaf	1
1	sprig thyme	1
10	peppercorns	10
4	stems parsley	4
1	clove garlic	1

1. Roast bones in 400°F/200°C oven until dark golden brown, about 1 hour. Remove bones from pan and place in stockpot with cold water. Bring to simmer. Skim off foam as needed.
2. Add vegetables to roasting pan and return to oven. Roast until lightly browned (approximately 15 minutes). Stir tomato paste into vegetables and roast another 5 minutes.
3. With kitchen twine, tie all bouquet garni ingredients into cheesecloth pouch.
4. Add vegetable and tomato mixture to stockpot. Add bouquet garni. Simmer for at least 4 hours and up to 8 hours, skimming as needed. Do not boil.
5. Strain stock. Cool and refrigerate. When cold, remove fat.
6. Return stock to pot and simmer until volume is reduced by half. Cool, then freeze or refrigerate for later use.

Yields 8 cups/2 L

Rich Pork Stock

Somehow pork adds richness to a stock without lending a distinctive taste. Try it in Winter Melon Soup (p. 18) and other noodle soup dishes. Soup bones can often be had for free or bought for a nominal price from your butcher.

3 lb	pork knuckle, rib or back bones, chopped	1.5 kg
2 lb	chicken necks and backs, chopped in 2-inch/5 cm chunks	1 kg
20 cups	cold water	5 L
1	onion, quartered	1
2	cloves garlic, whole	2
1	carrot, thickly sliced	1
3	large green onions, trimmed, cut in quarters	3
1-inch	piece ginger, thinly sliced	2.5 cm
1 tsp	white peppercorns	5 mL

1. Rinse chicken and pork bones thoroughly under cold running water. Add to large pot with cold water
2. Add all other ingredients. Over medium heat bring to slow boil, skimming off the foam and fat.
3. When stock starts to boil, reduce heat and keep at steady simmer for about 10 minutes. Continue skimming until surface of stock is mostly clear. Reduce heat to slow simmer, continue cooking for about 4 hours. Skim surface as necessary.
4. Strain finished stock through a fine-mesh sieve. Refrigerate and remove fat that solidifies on top. Freeze or refrigerate for later use.

Yields about 15 cups/3.75 L

FLAVOURINGS & EXTRAS

Five-spice Powder

Chinese five-spice powder is readily available in the spice section of most supermarkets, but if you want to make your own, try this.

8	star anise pods	8
2 tbsp	Szechuan peppercorns	25 mL
1 tbsp	ground cinnamon	15 mL
1 tbsp	ground cloves	15 mL
3 tbsp	ground fennel seeds	45 mL

1. Remove woody centres from star anise and grind remainder.
2. With mortar and pestle or in small container of blender, grind all spices together. Keep in glass container away from direct heat and light. Will keep for 1 month.

Curry Powder

If you'd rather buy ready-made curry powder, look for one labelled Madras curry powder. Madras curries most closely match the flavour of this one.

1 tbsp	ground chilies	15 mL
½ cup	ground coriander	125 mL
3 tbsp	ground cumin	45 mL
2 tsp	black mustard seeds*	10 mL
2 tsp	fenugreek seeds*	10 mL
1 tsp	ground black pepper	5 mL
2 tsp	ground turmeric	10 mL
4	curry leaves*	4

Grind all ingredients together.

Available where Indian foods and spices are sold.

Vietnamese-style Chili Sauce

Vietnamese-style chili sauce is available commercially, but it's easy to make if you can't find it in stores. More a paste than a sauce, it's hot with just a touch of sweetness. Seeds and bits of chili are still visible. This fresh-tasting chili sauce can be used in other dipping sauces or as a condiment on its own.

1 tbsp	canola oil	15 mL
6	habaneros or other hot chilies, seeded and diced	6
½ cup	minced shallots	125 mL
2 tbsp	brown sugar	25 mL
¼ cup	red wine vinegar	50 mL

1. Heat canola oil. Add chilies, shallots and brown sugar and saute for 5 minutes.
2. Add red wine vinegar to pan, stir and cook to reduce volume by half.
3. Pour into sterilized bottle and cap tightly. Will last indefinitely in refrigerator.

Yields about 1 cup/250 mL

Chili Care

When handling chilies, either wear rubber gloves or be very careful to wash your hands thoroughly. Do not touch your face or other sensitive parts of your body. If you do, try rubbing the area with some fresh lemon juice and rinsing thoroughly with cold water. If you touch your eyes, you may need to seek medical attention.

Tea Eggs and Chili Mayonnaise

See Photo, page 40

*For something as dramatic looking as these, they're very easy to make.
Chili Mayonnaise jazzes up the flavour. Serve them as appetizers with
Tea-smoked Seafood (p. 63) to get everyone in the mood for a party.
Quail eggs, if you can find them, are a wonderful variation on the theme.*

8	eggs	8
3 cups	water	750 mL
3 tbsp	Chinese black tea leaves	45 mL
1 tbsp	dark soy sauce	15 mL
1 tbsp	five-spice powder	15 mL

1. Put whole eggs gently into large saucepan and cover with cold water.
Over medium heat bring eggs slowly to boil, turn off heat and let stand
in hot water for 10 minutes. Remove and cool eggs thoroughly under
running water.
2. Gently crack eggshells by rolling on hard surface while pressing
lightly with palm, or by gently knocking with spoon. Shells should be
cracked but not broken or removed.
3. In saucepan, bring 3 cups/750 mL water to boil and add all other
ingredients. (Add 1 tsp/5 mL salt to water if you are not serving the chili
mayonnaise recipe below.) Reduce heat, add eggs and simmer gently for
30 minutes.
4. Remove from heat and let eggs stand in poaching liquid at least 30
minutes or overnight. Remove eggs from liquid and set aside to cool.
5. Shell eggs just before serving. Serve as is or with chili mayonnaise.

Chili Mayonnaise

½ cup	skim milk yogurt	125 mL
2 tbsp	low-fat mayonnaise	25 mL
1½ tsp	Vietnamese chili sauce, or to taste	7 mL
2 tbsp	finely chopped chives	25 mL
½ tsp	salt	2 mL

Mix all ingredients together. Spoon about 1 tsp/5 mL of chili mayonnaise onto an endive spear. Place ¼ tea egg, marbled side up, onto mayonnaise and serve as appetizer.

Serves 10

Each serving (including
mayonnaise) provides:

	Calories	75
g	Carbohydrates	2
g	Protein	6
g	Fat	5
g	Saturated Fat	1
mg	Cholesterol	171
g	Fibre	tr
mg	Sodium	285
mg	Potassium	89

Good: vitamin B-12

Candied Pecans with Sesame

The good news is these nuts are simply addictive. The bad news is the suggested servings are very small if you adhere to our HeartSmart guidelines. We have included this recipe because they are very good as a garnish for dishes such as Stir-fried Chicken with Mango (p. 76) or as an accompaniment for desserts such as the Poached Pears and Figs (p. 132). Use moderation. Our analysis is based on 14 pieces or 1½ ounces/43 grams nuts. Walnut halves also work well in this recipe.

	vegetable oil spray	
1 lb	shelled raw pecan or walnut halves	500 g
5 cups	water, divided	1.25 L
1 cup	sugar	250 mL
½ cup	honey	125 mL
¼ tsp	salt	1 mL
¼ cup	toasted sesame seeds	50 mL

1. Preheat oven to 275°F/140°C.
2. Lightly spray oil onto large cookie sheet and set aside.
3. If using walnuts, bring 4 cups water to boil, add walnuts and blanch for two minutes. Remove from heat, drain well, pat very dry and set aside. (Not necessary with pecans.)
4. In large skillet, combine remaining 1 cup/250 mL water, sugar, honey and salt and bring to boil. Continue to cook until syrupy. Reduce heat to medium and add nuts. Stir and boil for about 2 minutes, making sure that nuts are well coated.
5. Drain coated nuts in colander to remove excess syrup. Transfer nuts onto oiled cookie sheet, separate and spread evenly. Place in preheated oven and bake for about 30 minutes or until golden brown. Stir and turn nuts occasionally to ensure even cooking.
6. Remove from oven and cool slightly. While the nuts are still warm and tacky, toss in large bowl with the sesame seeds to coat. Spread out on cookie sheet again to cool and harden thoroughly. Serve alone or with other dishes, or store in glass jar with tight lid for snacks.

Serves 20

Each serving provides:

	Calories	229
g	Carbohydrates	22
g	Protein	2
g	Fat	17
g	Saturated Fat	1
mg	Cholesterol	0
g	Fibre	1
mg	Sodium	28
mg	Potassium	102

Top: *Fried Red Rice with Vegetables*, page 30 >
Bottom: *Singapore Stir-fried Noodles*, page 31 >

Basic Flavours

To make this book a simple, everyday adventure in oriental cuisine, keep these essential ingredients on hand: ginger, green onions, cilantro, soy sauce, fish sauce, hot bean paste, sesame oil, five-spice powder, dry sherry and an assortment of dried Chinese mushrooms. With these easy-to-find flavourings you can create most of the dishes in the book.

Glossary

While some of these Chinese ingredients may seem a little unusual or inaccessible, this glossary will show you where in the book to find detailed information and substitutes for each one. # corresponds to the photo identity and "See page…" guides you to more detailed information.

Explore the ethnic food sections of your supermarket or scout out local Chinese and Asian markets to find the ingredients listed.

Bok choy	# 2. Popular Chinese leafy green with fleshy white stalks.
Cellophane noodles	See page 110.
Chayote	# 11. See page 84.
Chinese almonds	Heart-shaped nuts, similar to bitter almonds.
Chinese celery	See page 100.
Chinese chives	# 15 and 21. See page 61.
Chinese eggplant	See page 119.
Chinese pickled cabbage	See page 24.
Chinese red dates	Dark red, tough-skinned dates mostly used in soups and desserts.
Cloud ear mushrooms	# 16 and 17. See page 21.
Daikon	# 8. See page 88.
Dried Chinese mushrooms	Black mushrooms that impart intense flavour when reconstituted.
Dried lily buds	# 22. See page 107.
Enoki mushrooms	# 14.
Fermented black beans	See page 70.
Fish sauce	See page 19.
Five-spice powder	See page 9.
Gai choy	# 5. See page 113.

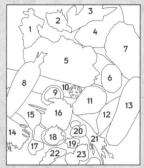

1: gai lan 2: bok choy (shown, bok choy sum, the heart of the mature bunch) 3: water spinach 4: winter melon 5: gai choy (mustard greens) 6: taro root 7: sui choy 8: white daikon 9: shiitake mushrooms 10: lotus root 11: chayote 12: see qua 13: mo qua 14: enoki mushrooms 15: Chinese chives, green and yellow 16: white cloud ear mushroom 17: dried cloud ear mushrooms 18: dried wood ear mushrooms 19: star anise 20: kumquats 21: Chinese flowering chives 22: dried lily buds 23: water chestnuts

< See legend (right) and glossary to identify ingredients

Gai lan	#1. See page 112.
Hoisin sauce	See page 98.
Hot bean paste	See page 100.
Japanese seven-spice	See page 45.
Jicama root	See page 122.
Kaffir lime leaves	See page 68.
Kumquats	# 20. Tiny citrus fruits with sweet skin and sour pulp.
Lemon grass	See page 68.
Lotus root	# 10. See page 107.
Mo qua	# 13. See page 96.
Oyster sauce	See page 52.
Pea sprouts	See page 120.
Pomelo	See page 74.
Red bean curd	See page 97.
Red miso paste	*(Sendai miso)* Japanese fermented soybean paste.
Red rice	Reddish brown, nutty flavoured long-grain rice.
Satay sauce	See page 86.
Sesame oil	Oil of toasted seeds, used to flavour fish, noodle and vegetable dishes.
See qua	# 12. See page 64.
Shanghai noodles	See page 32.
Star anise	# 19. Star-shaped woody pod with strong anise flavour.
Sui choy	# 7. See page 118.
Szechuan peppercorns	See page 49.
Taro root	# 6. See page 79.
Tofu skin wraps	See page 102.
Udon	See page 45.
Vietnamese chili sauce	See page 10.
Vietnamese rice wraps	Dried rice-pasta sheets commonly used for the famous salad rolls.
Water chestnuts	#23. See page 99.
Water spinach	# 3. See page 123.
Winter melon	# 4. See page 18.
Wonton/gyoza wrappers	Eggless pasta sheets.
Wood ear mushrooms	# 18. See page 33.
Yard-long beans	See page 75.

Winter Melon Soup

A classic summer soup that will keep you cool—your internal humours, that is. The Chinese believe that our health is governed by the balance of "hot" and "cold" elements in the body. Foods are classified as hot, cold or neutral depending on their supposed effects. For many Chinese people, the first reaction to illness is to alter their diet before consulting a physician.

"Balancing" considerations aside, you can substitute the meats in this soup with chicken, scallops or squid, or make a vegetarian version with a vegetable broth. Try using sea salt for seasoning if you don't want to use fish sauce, or create deeper flavour by adding the mushroom liquid.

Marinade:

1 tsp	fish sauce	5 mL
2 tsp	water	10 mL
½ tsp	sesame oil	2 mL
1 tsp	cornstarch	5 mL
2 oz	lean pork, cut in thin strips	60 g
6	large raw shrimp, coarsely chopped	6
1½ lb	winter melon or cucumber	750 g
1 oz	Chinese ham or prosciutto, finely diced	30 g
4	dried Chinese mushrooms, soaked and finely diced	4
6 cups	Chicken Stock (p. 3) or Rich Pork Stock (p. 8)	1.5 L

1. Combine marinade ingredients and marinate shrimp and pork strips for 10 minutes.
2. Remove soft pulp and seeds from winter melon. Cut away skin and reserve to flavour soup. Cut winter melon into ½-inch/1 cm cubes and set aside.
3. In large saucepan combine ham, mushrooms and stock and bring to boil. If using winter melon, add winter melon cubes and skin and bring to boil. Cook for 2 minutes covered. Reduce heat and simmer for 5 minutes covered, or until melon is tender. Remove melon skin and bring to boil.
4. Add shrimp and pork, boil for 1 more minute and serve. If using cucumber, add with shrimp and pork.

Serves 6

Tomato Eggplant Salmon Soup

This hearty, filling soup somehow manages to taste even better the next day. Serve it with steam buns for a satisfying lunch. Bulk it up with cooked cubed potatoes or leftover rice to serve as a snack or a light meal. For a variation, try making it with smoked salmon or different greens such as watercress or chrysanthemum. Cooked leftovers or odd cuts can also be used—it's a great way to use up your Christmas turkey!

6 cups	Chicken Stock (p. 3) or Vegetable Stock (p. 4)	1.5 L
3 lb	tomatoes, seeded, cut in 1-inch/2.5 cm cubes	1.5 kg
2	medium onions, diced	2
5	slices ginger	5
1½ lb	Chinese eggplant, cut in 1-inch/2.5 cm cubes	750 g
4 tsp	fish sauce	20 mL
1 tsp	white pepper	5 mL
1	egg, beaten, optional	1
¾ lb	fresh spinach, coarsely torn	375 g
¾ lb	salmon fillet, cut in 1-inch/2.5 cm cubes	375 g

1. In large pot, combine water or stock, tomatoes, onions and ginger slices and bring to boil. Reduce heat to medium and continue to simmer for 20 minutes.
2. Add eggplant, cover and simmer for 20 minutes.
3. Add fish sauce and season with white pepper. If using egg, pour in egg slowly while stirring soup to make egg swirls.
4. Turn off heat, add spinach and salmon. Cover and let stand for 5 minutes. Stir gently and serve immediately.

Serves 8

Fish Sauce
Nam pla, nuoc nam

This versatile flavouring, used widely in Southeast Asian cooking, is rich in vitamin B and protein. Its flavour is quite neutral compared to soy sauce, but it adds a rich, round taste to many dishes. I especially recommend it on vegetables. The ripe-cheese aroma dissipates in cooking.

Each serving provides:

	Calories	169
g	Carbohydrates	17
g	Protein	17
g	Fat	5
g	Saturated Fat	1
mg	Cholesterol	53
g	Fibre	6
mg	Sodium	329
mg	Potassium	1014

Excellent: vitamin A; vitamin D; vitamin B-6; vitamin B-12; folacin; fibre
Good: vitamin E; vitamin C; iron; riboflavin; niacin

White and Green Jade Soup

I discovered this simple, fresh soup while demonstrating Canadian cooking in Shanghai. The New Jin Jiang Hotel's original recipe calls for a local vegetable that resembles dandelion greens, but watercress or arugula works very well. The lightly cooked greens retain their peppery character while the soup has a beautiful silky texture.

Pork and Marinade:

¼ lb	lean pork, cut in thin strips	125 g
¼ tsp	salt	1 mL
pinch	white pepper	pinch
1 tbsp	dry sherry	15 mL
2 tsp	cornstarch	10 mL

Thickener:

1 tbsp	cornstarch	15 mL
2 tbsp	cold Chicken Stock (p. 3)	25 mL

½ lb	watercress, washed, trimmed	250 g
6 cups	Chicken Stock or Vegetable Stock (p. 4)	1.5 L
2 tsp	finely minced fresh ginger	10 mL
1 lb	soft tofu, drained and cut in ¼-inch/5 mm cubes	500 g
½ tsp	white pepper	2 mL
1 tsp	soy sauce	5 mL
2 tbsp	chopped green onion, optional	25 mL

1. Combine pork and marinade ingredients and marinate at least 30 minutes or overnight.
2. Combine cornstarch and cold chicken stock and set aside.
3. To blanch greens, bring 4 cups/1 L water to boil in large saucepan. Add watercress leaves and cook for about 1 minute or until bright green and just wilted. Run cold water over watercress. Drain, squeeze and finely chop leaves.
4. In large saucepan, bring stock to boil. Add ginger and pork and continue to boil for 1 minute. Skim off any foam.
5. Add tofu, return to boil and cook for 1 minute. Add thickening mixture and stir until soup is lightly thickened. Add chopped watercress and stir to mix while bringing to boil. Season with pepper and soy sauce. Remove from heat and sprinkle on green onions before serving.

Serves 6

Marinades

Marinating meat or fish brings out flavour. Cornstarch keeps it moist during cooking and retains the flavour of the marinade. If you anticipate that you will be short of time, you can cut and prepare a larger batch of meat and do the preliminary marinating a day or two ahead. When I was growing up, my mother would always have some beef, pork or chicken marinating so we kids could make a quick snack for ourselves before going out.

Each serving provides:

	Calories	95
g	Carbohydrates	3
g	Protein	11
g	Fat	5
g	Saturated Fat	1
mg	Cholesterol	12
g	Fibre	2
mg	Sodium	180
mg	Potassium	296

Excellent: vitamin E; iron
Good: thiamine

Corn and Shellfish Soup

This is a version of the soup that is on virtually every Cantonese restaurant menu. I've added the white cloud ear mushrooms for texture and substituted the usual green peas with asparagus to make it more interesting. Broccoli florets or stems make a good substitute.

Thickener:

1 tbsp	cornstarch	15 mL
2 tbsp	water or Chicken Stock (p. 3)	25 mL
⅓ cup	dried white cloud ear mushrooms	75 mL
6 cups	Chicken Stock or Rich Pork Stock (p. 8)	1.5 L
2 tsp	minced ginger	10 mL
1	19-oz/540 mL tin creamed corn	1
¼ lb	scallops, diced	125 g
¼ lb	crabmeat	125 g
1 cup	chopped asparagus	250 mL
1 tsp	sesame oil	5 mL
½ tsp	white pepper	2 mL
1	egg white, beaten	1

1. Mix cornstarch and water or stock and set aside.
2. Soak mushrooms in hot water for 15 minutes. Drain, trim off scaly bits and chop coarsely.
3. In large saucepan, bring chicken stock, ginger and mushrooms to boil over high heat for 1 minute. Reduce heat to medium. Add corn, scallops, crabmeat and asparagus and boil 2 minutes.
4. Season with sesame oil and pepper. Add cornstarch mixture, stir and cook until soup returns to boil and begins to thicken.
5. Remove from heat, pour in thin stream of beaten egg white while stirring the soup to form egg swirls. Serve.

Serves 6

Cloud Ears
White tree fungus

Dried white cloud ear mushrooms are sold in Chinese herbalists or grocery stores. Looking somewhat like loose sponges, they can be a bit bigger than a Ping-Pong ball and light brownish yellow to snow white. The large white ones are considered best. To prepare, simply soak them in warm water for 15 to 20 minutes and trim off the scaly bits at the base. They expand to more than 3 times the original volume.

Each serving provides:

	Calories	134
g	Carbohydrates	22
g	Protein	11
g	Fat	2
g	Saturated Fat	tr
mg	Cholesterol	21
g	Fibre	2
mg	Sodium	400
mg	Potassium	389

Excellent: folacin;
vitamin B-12
Good: zinc

Hot and Sour Chicken Soup

Chicken and Marinade:

¼ lb	skinless, boneless chicken breast, cut in thin strips	125 g
⅛ tsp	salt	0.5 mL
1 tbsp	dry sherry or Chinese cooking wine	15 mL
2 tsp	cornstarch	10 mL
½ cup	dried lily buds	125 mL
3	dried Chinese mushrooms	3

Flavouring:

1 tbsp	soy sauce	15 mL
1 tsp	sesame oil	5 mL
3 tbsp	cider vinegar or Chinese red vinegar	45 mL
½ tsp	pepper	2 mL
¼–½ tsp	Tabasco sauce	1–2 ml

Thickener:

1 tbsp	cornstarch	15 mL
2 tbsp	water	25 mL
6 cups	Chicken Stock (p. 3) or Shrimp Stock (p. 6)	1.5 L
½ cup	sliced button mushrooms	125 mL
1 lb	medium tofu, diced	500 mL
2 cups	young spinach leaves	500 mL
¼ cup	cilantro leaves	50 mL

1. Marinate chicken in marinade for 20 minutes or overnight.
2. Soak dried lily buds and dried mushrooms separately in 1 cup/250 mL hot water each for 15 minutes. Reserve and strain mushroom liquid; remove mushrooms and slice. Drain lily buds.
3. Combine flavouring ingredients except Tabasco sauce and set aside.
4. Combine thickener ingredients and set aside.
5. In large saucepan, combine mushroom liquid and stock and bring to boil over high heat. Add lily buds, Chinese mushrooms and sliced mushrooms and cook for 2 minutes. Add chicken and cook for 2 minutes. Add flavouring mixture and cook for 1 minute. Taste and add Tabasco and more vinegar according to taste.
6. Reduce heat to medium, add tofu and spinach and bring to boil, stirring gently to mix. Add thickening mixture and stir and cook until soup is lightly thickened. Garnish with cilantro leaves and serve immediately.

Serves 6

Each serving provides:		
	Calories	118
g	Carbohydrates	7
g	Protein	13
g	Fat	5
g	Saturated Fat	1
mg	Cholesterol	16
g	Fibre	2
mg	Sodium	253
mg	Potassium	314

Excellent: vitamin E; iron
Good: vitamin D; folacin; vitamin B-12

Fish Ball and Seaweed Soup

*This is a popular soup from Chiu Chow, the area in southern China
my parents came from. Preserved "winter" cabbage gives it a distinct
regional flavour. If you'd like to make it a stand-alone meal, add
cooked udon or rice noodles and adjust seasoning to taste.*

4 cups	Chicken Stock (p. 3) or Rich Pork Stock (p. 8)	1 L
3	slices ginger	3
1 tbsp	Chinese pickled cabbage, optional	15 mL
1	recipe Fish Balls (next page)	1
8 to 10	inner leaves of leaf lettuce	8 to 10
2	sheets toasted Japanese nori (*yakinori*) seaweed, cut in thin strips	2
2 tbsp	chopped cilantro leaves	25 mL
1 tsp	sesame oil, optional	5 mL

1. In saucepan, bring chicken stock to boil. Add ginger, pickled cabbage and fish balls and cook for 2 minutes.
2. Add lettuce leaves and nori and cook for 1 minute, stirring to mix.
3. Garnish with cilantro and sesame oil and serve.

Serves 4

Chinese Pickled Cabbage

Pickled vegetables, cured primarily with salt and made from vegetables of the mustard or cabbage families, are widely used as flavourings in Chinese cooking. My favourite brand is labelled Tianjin Preserved Vegetable and comes in an attractive potbellied crock with a plastic cap—net weight 600 grams. It adds great flavour to soups and vegetable dishes. Try it with green onions in an omelette.

Each serving provides:

	Calories	152
g	Carbohydrates	4
g	Protein	26
g	Fat	3
g	Saturated Fat	tr
mg	Cholesterol	45
g	Fibre	1
mg	Sodium	248
mg	Potassium	640

Excellent: vitamin B-12
Good: vitamin D; vitamin E; vitamin B-6; folacin

Fish Balls

I still have fond memories of Mother Chang, who came to the back gate of our school in Hong Kong with her little pushcart, rain or shine, proffering steaming fish balls dipped in soy sauce. Today, one can find many variants of this snack in Chinese restaurants, made from pork, beef, fish, shrimp and even cuttlefish.

This recipe can be formed into patties, fried in a non-stick pan with a bit of oil and served as fish cakes in stir-fries, in dumplings or by themselves.

1 tbsp	dried shrimp, optional	15 mL
2 tbsp	hot water	25 mL
1 lb	skinless fillet of red snapper or other white fish, coarsely chopped	500 g
1	egg white	1
2 tsp	cornstarch	10 mL
3 tbsp	finely chopped green onions	45 mL
1 tbsp	Ginger Juice (p. 48)	15 mL
1 tbsp	dry sherry	15 mL
½ tsp	white pepper	2 mL
¼ tsp	salt	1 mL

1. Soak dried shrimp in hot water until soft, about 30 minutes. Reserve liquid, drain shrimp and mince.
2. Combine all ingredients including shrimp liquid in food processor and blend until mixture becomes smooth, fine paste.
3. Put about 3 inches/8 cm cold water in large saucepan. Clean and wet hands and gently shape about ½ tbsp/7 mL of fish paste into ball. Place gently in cold water. Continue until paste is used up.
4. Bring water to boil slowly over medium-low heat. When fish balls rise to surface, remove with slotted spoon and place in ice water. Drain when thoroughly cooled. Fish balls can be stored covered for a day or two in the refrigerator.

Serves 4

Each serving provides:		
	Calories	130
g	Carbohydrates	2
g	Protein	25
g	Fat	2
g	Saturated Fat	tr
mg	Cholesterol	45
g	Fibre	tr
mg	Sodium	223
mg	Potassium	511

Excellent: vitamin B-12
Good: vitamin D;
vitamin B-6

Steamed Rice

All the dishes in this book are meant to be served with fluffy steamed rice. For a typical dinner for four, choose up to three dishes from the book, plus rice. In my house the rice pot is always simmering before I begin the final stages of cooking dinner.

This basic recipe uses a proportion of 1 part rice to 1⅓ parts water, which works well for long-grain, short-grain and red rice (or follow package instructions). Many Chinese people create their favourite blend. My personal best is a one-to-one ratio of jasmine rice from Thailand and short-grain rice from Japan. It combines the basmati-like fragrance of the jasmine rice and the chewy, starchy texture of the short-grain.

| 2 cups | long-grain rice or favourite blend | 500 mL |
| 2⅔ cups | cold water | 650 mL |

1. In heavy saucepan with tight-fitting lid, rinse rice in about 4 cups water, stirring to clean off any impurities and surface starch. Drain off water.
2. Add 2⅔ cups/650 mL water and bring mixture to boil over medium-high heat. Reduce heat to medium-low, cover and cook at high simmer for 20 minutes or until moisture is absorbed and rice looks fluffy. Adjust heat carefully during this stage and do not allow rice to boil over.
3. Remove from heat. Cover tightly and allow to stand for 10 minutes. Stir to loosen grains and serve.

Yields about 6 cups of cooked rice

Serves 6

Each serving provides:

	Calories	337
g	Carbohydrates	74
g	Protein	7
g	Fat	1
g	Saturated Fat	tr
mg	Cholesterol	0
g	Fibre	1
mg	Sodium	9
mg	Potassium	106

Gingered Brown Rice

Brown rice isn't popular in Chinese cooking as it's considered coarse and unrefined. But it's popular with me because of its nutty flavour and higher nutrient value. This particular recipe also gives it a richer flavour, making it ideal to accompany rich dishes like the Lamb Ossobuco Chinese Style (pp. 88-89). When lightly cooled, it's a good base for making sushi rolls.

2 cups	brown rice	500 mL
2⅓ cups	water	575 mL
2 tbsp	minced ginger	25 mL
1	large egg, beaten	1
2 tsp	Japanese rice vinegar	10 mL

1. Rinse and soak rice in cold water to cover for about 30 minutes. Drain.
2. In heavy saucepan, combine rice, water and ginger and bring to boil over high heat, partially covered. Reduce heat to low and simmer covered until liquid is absorbed, about 30 minutes.
3. Remove from heat and let stand to steam for 10 minutes. When rice is cooked, stir to loosen grains and stir in beaten egg until well mixed. Cover for another 5 minutes to allow egg to cook.
4. Add vinegar, stir to mix and serve.

Serves 4

Each serving provides:

	Calories	362
g	Carbohydrates	72
g	Protein	9
g	Fat	4
g	Saturated Fat	1
mg	Cholesterol	53
g	Fibre	3
mg	Sodium	23
mg	Potassium	237

Good: fibre; vitamin E; thiamine; niacin; vitamin B-6; zinc

29

Fried Red Rice with Vegetables

See photo, page 13

Fried rice is a great way to turn leftovers into a delicious one-pot dish. Your imagination is the limit. In general, cut the meat and vegetable ingredients into a small dice and make sure the rice is well cooled. Leftover rice is ideal, or use rice that is slightly undercooked: for best results use a bit less water to cook the rice if you are making it especially to go into a fried-rice dish.

I've chosen a combination of equal parts red and short-grain rice to give this dish colour and a wonderful crunchy texture.

2	large eggs, beaten	2
1 tbsp	canola oil	15 mL
1 tsp	minced garlic	5 mL
1 tsp	minced ginger	5 mL
5	dried Chinese mushrooms, soaked, drained and diced	5
1 cup	snow peas, trimmed, cut diagonally in 3 pieces	250 mL
¾ cup	diced carrot	175 mL
1 cup	sliced fresh mushrooms	250 mL
½ tsp	salt	2 mL
1 tbsp	Vegetable Stock (p. 4) or Chicken Stock (p. 3)	15 mL
4 cups	cooked red rice, cooled	1 L
¼ cup	Vegetable Stock or Chicken Stock	50 mL
1 tbsp	soy sauce	15 mL
½ cup	chopped green onion	125 mL
¼ tsp	black pepper	1 mL

1. Heat non-stick wok or skillet over medium heat. Cook eggs to make crepelike omelette. Turn over and cook other side briefly. Remove from pan and cut into ½-inch/1 cm squares. Set aside.

2. Add oil to wok or skillet over medium-high heat. Add all vegetables except green onions and stir-fry for 1 minute. Season with salt. Add the 1 tbsp/15 mL chicken stock and cover. Continue to cook for about 1 minute or until carrot is tender-crisp.

3. Add rice and stir-fry about 2 minutes, tossing until rice is well mixed, heated through and just starting to steam.

4. Add the ¼ cup/50 mL chicken stock plus soy sauce and stir well for 1 to 2 minutes until liquid is incorporated and rice is fluffy.

5. Add eggs and green onions and toss to mix. Season with pepper and serve.

Serves 4

Singapore Stir-fried Noodles

See photo, page 13

Obviously of Southeast Asian roots, this dish is now on the menus of Chinese restaurants everywhere. It's a good illustration of Chinese cooking as a growing craft—expanding and changing, ever eager to incorporate other ethnic influences in its repertoire.

½ lb	rice stick noodles (dry)	250 g
2	eggs, beaten	2
4 tsp	canola oil, divided	20 mL
⅓ lb	shelled small raw shrimp	170 g
¼ lb	Barbecued Pork (p. 97), cut in thin strips	125 g
¾ cup	celery, thinly sliced on the diagonal	175 mL
½ cup	chopped green onion	125 mL
2 tbsp	curry powder	25 mL
1 cup	Quick Thickened Stock (p. 2)	250 mL
1 tbsp	soy sauce	15 mL
2 cups	bean sprouts, tightly packed	500 mL
1 tbsp	chopped cilantro	15 mL
	pepper to taste	

1. Cover noodles with warm water and soak until soft, about 15 minutes. Drain and set aside.
2. Heat non-stick skillet over medium heat, pour in eggs and swirl to form thin layer on bottom. Flip eggs and cook other side briefly. Cut omelette into thin strips and set aside.
3. Heat 2 tsp/10 mL oil in large non-stick skillet or wok over high heat. Add shrimp and stir-fry for 1 minute. Add barbecued pork and celery and stir-fry for 1 minute. Remove from heat and stir in green onion and egg strips. Remove mixture from pan.
4. Heat remaining 2 tsp/10 mL oil in same pan over medium heat. Add curry powder and stir for 20 seconds. Add noodles and toss well. Add thickened stock and soy sauce and stir to mix well. Cover and cook for 2 minutes.
5. Add shrimp-and-pork mixture, mix well and cook over medium-high heat until moisture is completely absorbed. Add bean sprouts and toss to mix. Garnish with cilantro and season with freshly ground pepper if desired. Serve immediately.

Serves 4

Rice Stick Noodles

Sometimes called rice vermicelli, these come from China or Southeast Asia. They are white to off-white and usually sold dried and wrapped in plastic. They must be rehydrated before use—thicker ones in hot water and thin ones in cold water. Don't confuse them with mung bean noodles, popularly known as cellophane noodles, which are invariably thread-thin, almost transparent in the package and clear when cooked.

Each serving provides:

	Calories	361
g	Carbohydrates	47
g	Protein	19
g	Fat	11
g	Saturated Fat	2
mg	Cholesterol	177
g	Fibre	3
mg	Sodium	761
mg	Potassium	380

Excellent: iron; vitamin D; vitamin B-12

Good: zinc; thiamine; riboflavin; folacin; fibre

Peppered Beef with Shanghai Noodles

Shanghai Noodles

These eggless wheat noodles are a staple of northern China. Shanghai noodles are round and range from vermicelli- to udon-sized. I recommend the uncooked variety because they're coated with flour rather than oil to keep the strands from sticking. The thinner varieties are mostly used in soups and the thicker ones in noodle dishes. Fresh or dried pasta, especially fettuccine, will work very well in their place.

My love for pepper steak extends naturally to this Chinese version of the dish. As a noodle dish it makes a great lunch, but by all means try it without the noodles. Just double the beef and serve it over steamed rice.

Beef and Marinade:

½ lb	sirloin steak, trimmed of fat, cut in thin strips	250 g
1 tbsp	oyster sauce	15 mL
1½ tsp	soy sauce	7 mL
1 tsp	coarsely ground black pepper	5 mL
1½ tsp	cornstarch	7 mL

Sauce:

1 tbsp	soy sauce	15 mL
½ cup	Veal Demi-glace (p. 7) or Quick Thickened Stock (p. 2)	125mL
1 tsp	five-spice powder	5 mL
2 tbsp	dry sherry	25 mL

1 lb	uncooked Shanghai noodles or fettuccine	500 g
1 tbsp	canola oil	15 mL
3 tbsp	shallot, finely chopped	45 mL
4	cloves garlic, finely chopped	4
¾ cup	green bell pepper strips	175 mL
¾ cup	red bell pepper strips	175 mL
1 cup	bean sprouts, tightly packed	250 mL

1. Combine beef and marinade ingredients and marinate for 20 minutes.
2. Combine sauce ingredients and set aside.
3. Cook noodles in large pot of boiling water for 2 minutes (longer if using dried). Do not overcook. Rinse well in cold water, drain and set aside.
4. Heat non-stick wok or skillet over high heat and add oil. Add shallot and garlic and stir-fry for about 30 seconds. Add beef and stir-fry for 2 minutes, stirring to mix well and separate pieces. Add green and red bell peppers and stir-fry for 2 more minutes. Remove mixture from pan.
5. Add sauce mixture to pan and heat until simmering. Add noodles and stir constantly until heated through.
6. Add beef and pepper mixture and bean sprouts and mix well. Season with more freshly ground pepper if desired and serve.

Serves 4

Each serving provides:

	Calories	304
g	Carbohydrates	33
g	Protein	25
g	Fat	8
g	Saturated Fat	2
mg	Cholesterol	50
g	Fibre	3
mg	Sodium	664
mg	Potassium	465

Excellent: vitamin C; vitamin B-12; zinc

Good: fibre; folacin; iron

Spinach Fettuccine with Moo Shu Prawns

Moo Shu Pork is a famous dish from Shanghai, classically wrapped up in thin crepelike wheat pancakes. I came across this variation in a restaurant in Seattle's Chinatown. I have since tried it with a tomato-basil fettuccine, which also worked very well. Button or dried Chinese mushrooms can substitute for wood ears.

Flavouring:

¼ cup	dry sherry	50 mL
4 tsp	hoisin sauce	20 mL
4 tsp	fish sauce	20 mL
2 tbsp	water	25 mL
¾ lb	fresh spinach fettuccine	375 g
2	large eggs, beaten	2
1 tbsp	canola oil	15 mL
1 tbsp	finely chopped ginger	15 mL
1 tbsp	minced garlic	15 mL
¼ cup	dried wood ear mushrooms, soaked and coarsely chopped	50 mL
¼ cup	dried lily buds, soaked and torn in strips	50 mL
24	tiger prawns, shelled and deveined	24
1 cup	Quick Thickened Stock (p. 2)	250 mL
¼ tsp	pepper	1 mL
2 tbsp	chopped fresh cilantro	25 mL

1. Combine flavouring ingredients and set aside.
2. Cook fettuccine in large amount of boiling water until tender but firm. Rinse with cold water and drain. Set aside.
3. Heat large non-stick skillet or wok over medium heat. Cook eggs to make thin omelette. Turn over and cook other side briefly. Remove omelette, cut into thin strips and set aside.
4. Heat oil in same pan until just smoking. Add ginger, garlic, wood ears and lily buds and stir-fry for 30 seconds. Add prawns and stir-fry for about 2 minutes or until prawns turn pink and opaque. Remove mixture from pan.
5. Add thickened stock to pan. When simmering, add fettuccine and toss to heat through. Add flavouring mixture, egg strips and prawn mixture to pan and toss to mix well. Sprinkle with pepper and cilantro. Serve immediately.

Serves 4

Wood Ear Mushroom
Black tree fungus, black fungus

In Chinese medicine, this mushroom is considered to have positive effects on the circulatory system. As a culinary item it's used more for texture than taste. Wood ear and the similar cloud ear can be readily found in the dried food section of any Asian food store. To prepare them for cooking, soak them in hot water for about 20 minutes, then drain and trim off any tough scaly bits. They will expand to many times their size when rehydrated.

Each serving provides:

	Calories	303
g	Carbohydrates	36
g	Protein	17
g	Fat	7
g	Saturated Fat	1
mg	Cholesterol	208
g	Fibre	2
mg	Sodium	890
mg	Potassium	253

Excellent: vitamin D; vitamin B-12
Good: folacin; iron; thiamine; riboflavin; zinc

Steamed Chicken Dumplings

Two days before Chinese New Year, the kids' assembly line would be in full swing wrapping chiao-tsu *or dumplings. These delicious little parcels of meat and vegetables would be neatly lined up on trays in the refrigerator, ready to go into the soup pot, the steamer or the skillet when friends and relatives came calling.*

Dipping Sauce:

½ cup	Chinese black vinegar or balsamic vinegar	125 mL
2 tbsp	ginger peeled and cut in thin threads	25 mL

Dumplings:

1¼ lb	ground skinless chicken	625 g
1 tbsp	minced fresh ginger	15 mL
½ cup	finely chopped Chinese chives	125 mL
1 tsp	minced garlic	5 mL
1	7½-oz/213 mL tin water chestnuts, drained and finely chopped	1
2 tsp	sesame oil	10 mL
2 tbsp	soy sauce	25 mL
2 tbsp	dry sherry	25 mL
2 tbsp	Chicken Stock (p. 3)	25 mL
½ tsp	white pepper	2 mL
2 tsp	cornstarch	10 mL
1	package round wonton or gyoza wrappers	1
3	large carrots, thinly sliced, optional	3

1. Combine sauce ingredients and set aside.
2. Combine all dumpling ingredients down to cornstarch. Mix and stir vigorously in one direction for about 5 minutes to incorporate air into mixture.
3. Add cornstarch and mix well. Cover and refrigerate at least 30 minutes.
4. To make the dumplings, put about ½ tbsp/7 mL filling in centre of wrapper. Dampen inside edge of wrapper. Fold wrapper in half over filling to make parcel. Seal edge and pinch into a few small pleats. Repeat procedure with balance of ingredients to make 25 to 30 dumplings.
5. Heat steamer over medium heat. Either brush steamer rack lightly with oil or place carrot slice under each dumpling to prevent sticking. Space dumplings in one layer in steamer and steam in small lots, 7 to 8 minutes for each batch. Serve dumplings hot with dipping sauce.

Serves 6

Each serving provides:

	Calories	449
g	Carbohydrates	51
g	Protein	36
g	Fat	10
g	Saturated Fat	2
mg	Cholesterol	91
g	Fibre	1
mg	Sodium	864
mg	Potassium	411

Excellent: thiamine; riboflavin; niacin; iron
Good: vitamin B-6; zinc

Boiled Pork Dumplings

Although I doubt that they are the actual predecessor of the Italian ravioli, chiao-tsu provide the inventive cook the same latitude for creative expression. If chicken or pork doesn't tickle your fancy, try coarsely chopped shrimp with Chinese chives, salmon with ginger and scallions or even mashed potatoes with green peas and carrots.

Dipping Sauce:

1 tsp	sesame oil	5 mL
1 1/2 tsp	Vietnamese chili sauce or hot bean sauce	7 mL
1/4 cup	Chinese red vinegar or cider vinegar	50 mL

Dumplings:

1/4 cup	dried wood ear mushrooms, soaked and thinly sliced	50 mL
1 lb	minced lean pork	500 g
1 tbsp	peeled and finely grated ginger	15 mL
1/4 cup	chopped green onions	50 mL
1/2 tsp	minced garlic	2 mL
1 tsp	salt	5 mL
1 tbsp	dry sherry	15 mL
1 tbsp	Chicken Stock (p. 3)	15 mL
1/2 tsp	white pepper	2 mL
2 tsp	cornstarch	10 mL
1 cup	finely chopped sui choy (Napa cabbage) or savoy cabbage leaves, tightly packed	250 mL
1	package round wonton or gyoza wrappers	1

1. Combine sauce ingredients and set aside.
2. Combine all dumpling ingredients except wrappers and mix well.
3. To make dumplings, put 1/2 tbsp/7 mL filling in centre of wrapper. Dampen inside edge of the wrapper and fold in half over filling to make parcel. Seal edge and pinch into a few small pleats. Repeat procedure with balance of ingredients to make 25 to 30 dumplings.
4. Half-fill large pot with water (about 16 cups/4 L) and bring to boil over high heat. Add dumplings, stirring gently to prevent sticking. When they float to surface, add about 1 cup/250 mL cold water. When they float to top again, repeat. When dumplings float to top a third time, test for doneness.
5. Remove dumplings with slotted spoon and serve hot with dipping sauce.

Serves 6

Each serving provides:

	Calories	347
g	Carbohydrates	47
g	Protein	25
g	Fat	6
g	Saturated Fat	2
mg	Cholesterol	54
g	Fibre	1
mg	Sodium	858
mg	Potassium	465

Excellent: thiamine; riboflavin; niacin; vitamin B-12; iron; zinc
Good: vitamin B-6

Chicken Noodle Rolls

These make impressive appetizers or a satisfying lunch. You can refrigerate the filling ahead of time, then make the rolls and steam them at the last minute.

| 6 | dried Chinese mushrooms | 6 |
| 1/2 cup | hot water | 125 mL |

Chicken and Marinade:

1/2 lb	boneless chicken breast, cut in thin strips	250 g
2 tsp	dry sherry	10 mL
2 tsp	cornstarch	10 mL

Filling:

1 1/2 tsp	canola oil	7 mL
2 tsp	minced ginger	10 mL
1 tsp	hot red pepper flakes	5 mL
2 cups	Chinese chives, cut in 2-inch/5 cm lengths	500 mL
1 cup	bamboo shoots, cut in matchsticks	250 mL

Sauce:

1/4 cup	mushroom liquid	50 mL
1 1/2 tsp	oyster sauce	7 mL
1 1/2 tsp	soy sauce	7 mL

8 sheets	8-inch/20 cm round Vietnamese rice wraps	8
1 tsp	sesame oil	5 mL
1 tbsp	toasted garlic and onion flakes (p. 122, step 2)	15 mL
1 tbsp	finely chopped green onion, optional	15 mL

1. Soak dried mushrooms in hot water for 20 minutes. Reserve and strain liquid. Remove mushrooms and slice into thin strips.

2. Combine chicken and marinade ingredients and set aside.

3. Heat oil in non-stick skillet or wok over medium-high heat. Add ginger, hot pepper flakes and chicken and stir-fry for 1 minute. Add all vegetables including mushrooms and continue to stir-fry for 2 minutes. Add sauce ingredients and continue to cook until liquid is mostly absorbed. Transfer to bowl and cool slightly.

4. Heat steamer over boiling water. Lightly brush large plate with some sesame oil.

5. To make rolls, half-fill large bowl with boiling or very hot water. When filling is ready, dip each Vietnamese rice wrap in hot water for 3 to 5 seconds until just softened. Remove with tongs and place sheet on flat dry surface. Spoon 2 to 3 tbsp/25 to 45 mL of filling mixture onto bottom half of sheet. Fold bottom and side edges over filling and roll tightly. Place seam-side down on oiled plate and brush lightly with sesame oil. Repeat with remaining sheets and filling to make eight 6-inch/15 cm rolls.

6. Place plate with rolls in steamer and steam for 3 minutes. Sprinkle with green onions and garlic and onion flakes if desired. With scissors, cut rolls crosswise into four bite-sized pieces before serving.

Serves 4

Rolling Instructions

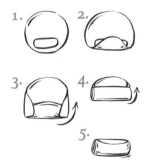

Each serving provides:
	Calories	229
g	Carbohydrates	28
g	Protein	17
g	Fat	5
g	Saturated Fat	1
mg	Cholesterol	34
g	Fibre	2
mg	Sodium	428
mg	Potassium	362

Excellent: vitamin D;
niacin
Good: vitamin B-6;
folacin; zinc

Steamed Chicken Buns

Dough:

2 ½ cups	all-purpose flour	625 mL
3 ½ tsp	baking powder	17 mL
3 tbsp	icing sugar	45 mL
2 tbsp	canola oil	25 mL
¾ cup	lukewarm water	175 mL
½ tsp	white vinegar	2 mL
10	3-inch/8 cm squares waxed or parchment paper	10

Filling:

1 ¼ lb	ground skinless chicken	625 g
1 tbsp	peeled and finely grated ginger	15 mL
½ cup	finely chopped Chinese chives	125 mL
1 tsp	minced garlic	5 mL
1	7 ½-oz/213 mL tin water chestnuts, drained and finely chopped	1
2 tsp	sesame oil	10 mL
2 tbsp	soy sauce	25 mL
2 tbsp	dry sherry	25 mL
2 tbsp	Chicken Stock (p. 3) or Rich Pork Stock (p. 8)	25 mL
½ tsp	white pepper	2 mL
2 tsp	cornstarch	10 mL

1. Sift together flour and baking powder. Stir in icing sugar and rub in oil with fingertips until evenly distributed. Combine water and vinegar and add slowly to flour mixture, mixing well. Knead to form fairly soft dough. Shape dough into smooth ball, cover and allow to rest for 30 minutes.
2. Meanwhile, combine all filling ingredients, mix well and refrigerate.
3. To make buns, divide dough into 10 portions and mould each into smooth ball. Roll out on lightly floured board to 4-inch/10 cm circle. Put spoonful of filling in centre of circle and gather edges towards middle. Fold, pleat and pinch dough to seal. Place each bun gathered-side down on square of parchment paper. Repeat procedure with balance of ingredients.
4. Heat steamer over boiling water. Space buns in steamer, cover and steam for 20 minutes. Serve warm. Cooked buns can be refrigerated overnight and reheated by steaming for 3 minutes before serving.

Serves 10

Each serving provides:

	Calories	274
g	Carbohydrates	28
g	Protein	20
g	Fat	8
g	Saturated Fat	2
mg	Cholesterol	51
g	Fibre	1
mg	Sodium	221
mg	Potassium	199

Excellent: niacin

Good: thiamine; riboflavin; vitamin B-6; iron; zinc

Pan-roasted Snapper Fillets with Chinese Ratatouille, page 54 >

Prawn Toast

My kids can never have enough of these favourite dim sum items. Traditionally they are deep-fried, but this baking method works just as well. These tasty tidbits vanished from my kitchen table before I had a chance to offer any to Nancy Ling, our dietitian for this book.

6	slices sandwich bread	6

Shrimp Mixture:

¾ lb	peeled and cleaned raw prawns	375 g
1	egg white	1
½ tsp	salt	2 mL
¼ tsp	white pepper	1 mL
1½ tsp	cornstarch	7 mL
1 tbsp	finely chopped cilantro	15 mL
2 tbsp	finely chopped Chinese chives	25 mL
2 tsp	minced ginger	10 mL
2 tbsp	mirin or medium sherry	25 mL
½ cup	water chestnuts, chopped	125 mL
2 tsp	sesame oil, divided	10 mL
1 tsp	honey, optional	5 mL

1. Preheat oven to 250°F/120°C. Cut crust from bread slices. Cut slices diagonally into quarters. Toast triangles on baking sheet for 20 minutes or until bread is crisp.
2. Preheat broiler to high and place rack about 6 inches/15 cm from heat.
3. In food processor, pulse all shrimp mixture ingredients except water chestnuts until thick, coarse paste is formed. Add water chestnuts and pulse two or three times briefly to mix.
4. Heap spoonful of shrimp mixture onto each toast triangle and spread mixture to edge.
5. Line baking sheet with foil and brush on 1 tsp/5 mL of the sesame oil evenly. Space shrimp toasts on baking sheet and broil for 3 to 4 minutes or until shrimp paste feels firm.
6. With remaining sesame oil, brush top of each toast. Broil for 2 more minutes and serve while hot. Or, if you plan on serving cold, mix in 1 tsp/5 mL honey for the final basting to prevent drying out.

Makes 24 pieces, serves 6 as appetizer

Each serving provides:

	Calories	169
g	Carbohydrates	19
g	Protein	15
g	Fat	3
g	Saturated Fat	1
mg	Cholesterol	111
g	Fibre	1
mg	Sodium	459
mg	Potassium	175

Excellent: vitamin D, riboflavin; vitamin B-12
Good: iron

< *Tea-smoked Seafood and Tea Eggs*, pages 63 and 11

Taro-stuffed Green Peppers

Mushroom Liquid

The liquid from soaking Chinese mushrooms is very flavourful and should be kept to use as a simple stock whenever possible. Just let it settle for a minute or two and pour off the top two-thirds for use. Discard the bottom one-third if it has any dirt or impurities in it.

A versatile dish that can be served with steamed rice or as a garnish for a western-style meal. Use potatoes if you can't find taro root. Yukon Golds are great. Oriental vegetables such as bamboo shoots or water chestnuts can be used too.

4	dried Chinese mushrooms	4
1/2 cup	hot water	125 mL

Mashed Taro:

1–1 1/2 lb	taro root or potatoes, peeled and sliced	500-750 g
1/2 tsp	salt	2 mL
1/2 tsp	five-spice powder	2 mL

Sauce:

1 tbsp	soy sauce	15 mL
1/4 cup	Vegetable Stock (p. 4)	50 mL
1/4 cup	mushroom liquid	50 mL
2 tsp	cornstarch	10 mL
1/2 tsp	white pepper	2 mL

2 tsp	canola oil	10 mL
2 tsp	minced ginger	10 mL
2 tbsp	finely chopped onions	25 mL
1 cup	frozen peas	250 mL
1/2 cup	finely diced carrots	125 mL
1 cup	corn kernels	250 mL

4	green bell peppers, quartered and seeded	4
1 tsp	sesame oil	5 mL

1. Soak dried mushrooms in hot water for 20 minutes. Reserve and strain liquid; remove and finely dice mushrooms.

2. Steam taro slices until tender, about 15 minutes. Mash taro with salt and five-spice powder until smooth.

3. Combine sauce ingredients and set aside.

4. Preheat oven to 375°F/190°C.

5. Heat non-stick skillet or wok over medium-high heat. Add oil, ginger and onions and saute for 1 minute or until onions are golden. Add all vegetables except green peppers and stir to mix for 1 minute. Add sauce mixture and bring to boil. Stir until sauce is thickened and mostly absorbed. Set aside.

6. Place a heaping spoonful of vegetable filling in each quarter of green pepper. Top with enough mashed taro root to cover filling and green pepper to edges. Brush lightly with sesame oil.

7. Bake stuffed peppers in oven for 15 minutes or until peppers are tender and taro is golden. Serve.

Serves 6

Each serving provides:		
	Calories	176
g	Carbohydrates	37
g	Protein	4
g	Fat	3
g	Saturated Fat	tr
mg	Cholesterol	0
g	Fibre	7
mg	Sodium	391
mg	Potassium	688

Excellent: vitamin A;
vitamin C; fibre; folacin
Good: vitamin D;
thiamine; vitamin B-6

43

Chicken Congee

Whenever I get sick or have a cold, congee (rice porridge) is the only thing that makes me feel better. Among my favourite kinds are chicken, fish and one made from pork and "century old" eggs. Firm whitefish slices such as lingcod or snapper can substitute for the chicken. Other seafood, pork or beef can be used as well.

Chicken and Marinade:

¾ lb	boneless, skinless chicken breast or thigh, thinly sliced	375 g
1 tbsp	cornstarch	15 mL
1 tbsp	dry sherry	15 mL
½ tsp	salt	2 mL
¼ tsp	white pepper	1 mL

Congee:

1 cup	short-grain rice	250 mL
10 cups	water	2.5 L
1 cup	Chicken Stock (p. 3) or Rich Pork Stock (p. 8)	250 mL
1 tbsp	grated ginger, or to taste	15 mL
1 tsp	sesame oil, for garnish	5 mL
2 tbsp	chopped green onions, for garnish	25 mL

1. Combine chicken and marinade ingredients, mix well and set aside.
2. To make congee, combine rice and water in large pot and bring to boil over high heat. Don't allow it to boil over at any point. Turn heat to medium-low and simmer partially covered for about 1½ hours or until rice grains are broken and almost dissolved and mixture has texture of thin porridge. While simmering, stir occasionally to prevent sticking and burning.
3. To serve congee, add chicken stock to congee and bring to vigorous boil. Add ginger and marinated chicken slices, stir to mix and allow to boil for 2 minutes or until chicken is cooked.
4. Divide congee into equal portions in soup bowls. Garnish each with a drop or two of sesame oil and a sprinkling of green onions.

Serves 4

Each serving provides:

	Calories	333
g	Carbohydrates	45
g	Protein	21
g	Fat	6
g	Saturated Fat	1
mg	Cholesterol	54
g	Fibre	1
mg	Sodium	320
mg	Potassium	209

Excellent: niacin

Good: thiamine; vitamin B-6; iron; zinc

Assorted Meats with Udon in Soup

5 cups	Chicken Stock (p. 3) or Chinese-style Vegetable Stock (p. 5)	1.25 L
1 tbsp	soy sauce	15 mL
1 tsp	sesame oil	5 mL
1 tbsp	dried shrimp, toasted	15 mL
1 tbsp	Chinese pickled cabbage	15 mL
3	slices ginger	3
1 lb	instant or cooked udon noodles or spaghetti	500 g
¼ lb	Barbecued Pork (p. 97), sliced	125 g
2	hard-cooked or Tea Eggs (p. 11), halved	2
4	stems gai lan or bok choy, cut in 2-inch/5 cm lengths	4
8	tiger prawns, shelled and deveined	8
6	large scallops, cut crosswise in 3 slices	6
4	baby cuttlefish or squid, rinsed and cleaned	4
1 tsp	Japanese seven-spice, optional	5 mL

1. Combine chicken stock, soy sauce and sesame oil and bring to boil. Add dried shrimp, pickled cabbage and ginger and cook for 1 minute.

2. Add noodles and cook, stirring to separate noodles for 2 minutes or until noodles are heated through. Remove from broth and drain; transfer noodles to soup tureen or separate bowls. Arrange pork slices and egg halves on noodles.

3. Add gai lan or bok choy to broth, bring to boil and cook for 1 minute. Add all seafood, bring to boil and continue cooking for 2 minutes.

4. Pour soup into tureen or bowls, briefly arrange seafood and vegetables attractively, garnish with sprinkling of seven-spice if desired and serve.

Serves 4

Udon

These thick Japanese wheat noodles come precooked in vacuum packages or uncooked and loose. For uncooked udon, blanch it in boiling water according to manufacturer's instructions and drain. Thick spaghetti is a substitute.

Japanese Seven-spice
Shichimi togarashi

This mixture typically includes seven dried ingredients such as ground togarashi peppers, Szechuan pepper, mandarin orange peel, sesame seeds, nori seaweed, black hemp seeds and others in different combinations. If you can't find it, mix equal parts black and Szechuan peppercorns and grind as you need.

Each serving provides:

	Calories	314
g	Carbohydrates	36
g	Protein	26
g	Fat	7
g	Saturated Fat	2
mg	Cholesterol	134
g	Fibre	2
mg	Sodium	713
mg	Potassium	267

Excellent: vitamin A; vitamin C; riboflavin; niacin; vitamin B-6; folacin; vitamin B-12; calcium; iron
Good: vitamin B-1

Baked Chicken Chow Mein

This is like the crisp chow mein served in Chinese restaurants but without all the fat. The steamed noodles called for in this recipe are widely available in supermarkets. Thin dried egg noodles, mostly sold in small cakes, will work as well. Cook them, then dry very well before baking.

Chicken and Marinade:

1 lb	boneless chicken breast, cut in thin strips	500 g
1 tbsp	soy sauce	15 mL
¼ tsp	salt	1 mL
1 tbsp	dry sherry	15 mL
¼ tsp	white pepper	1 mL
1 tbsp	cornstarch	15 mL
1 lb	Chinese-style steamed noodles or cooked thin egg noodles	500 g
1½ cups	Chicken Stock (p. 3)	375 mL
1 tbsp	minced ginger	15 mL
½ cup	thinly sliced onions	125 mL
3	large dried Chinese mushrooms, soaked and thinly sliced	3
2 cups	Chinese flowering chives or green onions, cut in quarters	500 mL
2 tsp	sesame oil	10 mL
3 cups	bean sprouts, tightly packed	750 mL
	black pepper to taste	

1. Combine chicken and marinade ingredients, mix well and set aside.
2. Blanch noodles in large amount of boiling water for 1 minute or as per package instructions. Drain well and cool slightly. Fluff up noodles to allow drying. When dried, spread noodles loosely on large cookie sheet lined with aluminum foil.
3. Heat oven broiler to medium-high. Broil noodles for about 5 minutes on each side, checking frequently, until crisped but not burned. Keep warm.
4. Meanwhile, heat wok over high heat, add stock and bring to boil. Add ginger, onions and mushrooms and cook for 1 minute. Add chicken and cook for 2 minutes. Stock should thicken slightly. Add flowering chives and sesame oil; stir to mix for 1 minute. (If using green onions, cook for only 30 seconds.)
5. Remove from heat. Stir in bean sprouts. Season with pepper. Pour chicken mixture over noodles and serve.

Serves 4

Each serving provides:

	Calories	358
g	Carbohydrates	43
g	Protein	33
g	Fat	6
g	Saturated Fat	1
mg	Cholesterol	100
g	Fibre	5
mg	Sodium	466
mg	Potassium	555

Excellent: vitamin D; thiamine; riboflavin; niacin; vitamin B-6; folacin; iron
Good: fibre; vitamin C; vitamin B-12; zinc

Salmon Roulades with Enoki Mushrooms

Coral-coloured salmon wrapped around white, threadlike enoki mushrooms and tied up with a strand of green onion—these are as dramatic as they are delicious. You can try this with other combinations too, like sole or trout wrapped around thin green asparagus or blanched carrot matchsticks.

Salmon and Marinade:

¾ lb	salmon fillets	375 g
1 tbsp	Ginger Juice (see sidebar)	15 mL
¼ tsp	salt	1 mL
2 tsp	cornstarch	10 mL
1	egg white, lightly beaten	1
1 to 2	bunches green onions, green parts only	1 to 2
2	3½-oz/100 g pkgs enoki mushrooms	2

Sauce:

1 tbsp	soy sauce	15 mL
3 tbsp	Chicken Stock (p. 3)	45 mL
1 tsp	sesame oil	5 mL
2 tbsp	sake or dry sherry	25 mL
pinch	sugar	pinch

1. Using sharp knife, slice each salmon fillet across grain into thin slabs. Cut slabs into 2-by-4-inch/5-by-10 cm rectangles. Marinate fish pieces with marinade for 10 minutes.
2. In boiling water, blanch green parts from green onions until just wilted, about 30 seconds. Run under cold water until thoroughly cooled. Reserve in ice water. Have a strand for every fish slice and a few to spare.
3. Trim enoki mushrooms and separate into small bundles, one per fish slice.
4. Roll each bundle of mushrooms in fish slice with tops of mushrooms showing. Tie green onion around middle of each roll and trim. Arrange fish bundles on lightly oiled plate.
5. Place plate of fish in steamer over boiling water, cover tightly and steam for about 3 minutes or until fish flakes easily. Or microwave covered with plastic wrap for 2 minutes, loosen covering and allow to rest 1 minute.
6. Meanwhile, combine sauce ingredients and bring to boil. Pour sauce over fish rolls and serve immediately. Garnish with cilantro sprigs if desired.

Serves 4

Ginger Juice

Place small knobs of peeled ginger in a sturdy garlic press and press to extract juice. Or place small knobs or slices of ginger in a food processor or blender with enough water to start a puree and blend until liquefied. Strain through a layer of cheesecloth, squeezing thoroughly to extract as much liquid as possible, and discard the solids. For seafood dishes, use white wine or dry sherry as the liquid.

Each serving provides:

	Calories	210
g	Carbohydrates	7
g	Protein	26
g	Fat	8
g	Saturated Fat	2
mg	Cholesterol	48
g	Fibre	tr
mg	Sodium	452
mg	Potassium	629

Excellent: vitamin D; niacin; vitamin B-12

Good: vitamin E; riboflavin; vitamin B-6

Salmon with Szechuan Pepper

I have adapted my parents' favourite hometown chicken dish for salmon. It's also wonderful made with prawns, and delicious with other firm white fish such as snapper, cod or even squid. It's traditionally garnished with a deep-fried herb that tastes like basil. The fresh sprout mixture here gives it that contrasting crunch without the fat.

Salmon and Marinade:

¾ lb	skinless salmon fillets, cut in bite-sized slices	375 g
1 tsp	dark or mushroom soy sauce (for colour)	5 mL
1 tsp	oyster sauce	5 mL
1½ tsp	soy sauce	7 mL
½ tsp	pepper	2 mL
½ tsp	sesame oil	2 mL
2 tsp	cornstarch	10 mL
1 tbsp	water	15 mL

Garnish:

1 cup	bean sprouts	250 mL
1 cup	radish sprouts	250 mL
1 cup	pea sprouts	250 mL
2 tsp	Szechuan peppercorns, whole	10 mL
1 tbsp	canola oil	15 mL
1	clove garlic, minced	1
2 tbsp	chopped shallots	25 mL
2 tbsp	dry sherry	25 mL
3 tbsp	Chicken Stock (p. 3) or Shrimp Stock (p. 6)	45 mL
	juice of half a lemon	

1. Marinate salmon with marinade ingredients for 10 minutes.
2. Toss sprouts together and arrange in ring around large plate, leaving room in centre for cooked salmon.
3. In dry skillet, toast Szechuan peppercorns over medium heat until fragrant. Crush into coarse grains. Reserve.
4. Heat oil in non-stick skillet or wok over medium-high heat. Saute salmon slices for about 1 minute on each side. Add Szechuan pepper, garlic and shallots and toss to mix for 30 seconds. Add sherry and continue cooking until liquid is absorbed. Add stock, stir and cook until sauce is thickened and salmon is well coated. Place salmon in centre of garnished plate, squeeze lemon on fish and serve.

Serves 4

Szechuan Peppercorns

These dried reddish-brown berries native to Szechuan province have a spicy fragrance not unlike junipers, and a curiously distinctive numbing effect on the tongue when raw. I like to keep a combination of equal amounts of black and Szechuan peppercorns in my cooking grinder. It's a versatile combo of earthiness and heat.

Each serving provides:

	Calories	265
g	Carbohydrates	15
g	Protein	28
g	Fat	11
g	Saturated Fat	2
mg	Cholesterol	25
g	Fibre	2
mg	Sodium	326
mg	Potassium	616

Excellent: vitamin D; niacin; vitamin B-6; folacin; vitamin B-12

Good: thiamine; riboflavin; iron

Steamed Whole Rockfish

A whole fish is a must at a Chinese New Year banquet. It signifies abundance and completeness. Instead of rockfish, which is a West Coast specialty, try using any fish small enough to fit into your wok or steamer. For less festive occasions, fish fillets or steaks will do. The appealing combination of ginger and sherry is a classic Chinese accompaniment for fish—the equivalent of lemon in western cooking.

3	green onions	3
1½ lb	whole rockfish, cleaned and scaled (leave head and tail on)	750 g
1 tbsp	dry sherry	15 mL
2 tbsp	shredded fresh ginger	25 mL
1 tbsp	Chicken Stock (p. 3)	15 mL
1 tbsp	soy sauce	15 mL
1 tsp	sesame oil	5 mL
6	cilantro sprigs	6

1. Smash 2 of the whole green onions and cut each in half crosswise; place on heatproof platter that will fit into steamer. Place fish on top of onions and pour sherry evenly over fish. Sprinkle with shredded ginger. Place in steamer and steam for 8 minutes or until fish flakes easily.
2. Meanwhile, cut remaining green onion into matchsticks and set aside.
3. In small saucepan, heat chicken stock, soy sauce and sesame oil until just heated through.
4. When fish is cooked, transfer fish and juices onto serving platter; discard cooked green onions. Sprinkle fish with matchstick green onion. Pour stock mixture over fish. Garnish with fresh cilantro sprigs if desired and serve immediately.

Serves 4

Steamers

Common types of steamers are made from bamboo, steel or aluminum. Bamboo ones with lids are designed to sit in a wok at least 3 inches/8 cm larger in diameter. Metal ones often come with their own shallow pots for water. But if space is at a premium, look for round bamboo or metal racks that fit nicely into your wok. In a pinch, a small cake rack will do the trick. And failing that, set two wooden chopsticks a few inches apart in your wok, then balance a platter on them. You'll need a dome-shaped lid for your wok to allow the steam to circulate.

Each serving provides:

	Calories	155
g	Carbohydrates	1
g	Protein	28
g	Fat	3
g	Saturated Fat	1
mg	Cholesterol	49
g	Fibre	0
mg	Sodium	346
mg	Potassium	628

Excellent: vitamin B-12
Good: niacin; vitamin B-6

Pan-fried Sole Fillets with Mustard Greens and Mushrooms

Any combination of mushrooms may be used here. In fact the different sizes and shapes make the dish more interesting. If you use canned mushrooms, look for Chinese straw mushrooms. Place them in a sieve and rinse them in cold water to remove some of the extra salt.

Fish and Marinade:

1 lb	sole fillets, cut into 2-inch/5 cm pieces	500 g
1 tsp	fish sauce	5 mL
1 tbsp	cornstarch	15 mL
2	egg whites, lightly beaten	2
1 tbsp	canola oil	15 mL
6	cloves garlic, whole, peeled	6
½ cup	Quick Thickened Stock (chicken or shrimp)(p. 2)	125 mL
1 tbsp	dry sherry	15 mL
6	thin slices ginger	6
1	carrot, sliced thinly	1
1 lb	mustard green stalks, cut diagonally in 1½-inch/4 cm lengths	500 g
1 tsp	soy sauce	5 mL
2	green onions, cut in quarters	2
2 cups	small oyster mushrooms, trimmed	500 mL
	white pepper to taste	

1. Combine fish with marinade ingredients and set aside for 10 minutes.
2. Heat non-stick wok or skillet to medium-high. Add oil, then add garlic and saute for 1 minute or until golden brown. Remove and set aside.
3. Add fish pieces and pan-fry for about 30 seconds on each side or until just undercooked. Remove and keep warm.
4. Add thickened stock and sherry to pan and bring to boil. Add ginger, carrots and mustard greens and stir to mix. Cover and cook over medium heat for 2 minutes or until greens are just tender.
5. Add soy sauce, green onions and mushrooms; stir to mix and cook for 1 minute. Meanwhile, cut sauteed garlic into thin slices. Add fish pieces and garlic slices to pan. Toss gently to mix and cook until liquid is mostly absorbed. Remove ginger slices if you wish. Season with pepper and serve immediately.

Serves 4

Egg Whites

Egg whites are often used in marinades. They help the food retain moisture and give it a silky texture without adding cholesterol or fat. In some areas you can buy fresh egg whites in plastic bottles at supermarket dairy cases.

Oyster Mushrooms

These tasty, fan-shaped mushrooms sometimes come in bright yellow and pink. These are dyed and lose their colour when cooked, so I recommend staying with the natural ones.

Each serving provides:

	Calories	220
g	Carbohydrates	13
g	Protein	30
g	Fat	5
g	Saturated Fat	1
mg	Cholesterol	60
g	Fibre	3
mg	Sodium	359
mg	Potassium	863

Excellent: vitamin A; vitamin D; vitamin E; vitamin C; folacin; vitamin B-12
Good: fibre; riboflavin; niacin

51

Steamed Halibut and Lettuce Rolls

An elegant, delicate and nutritious twist on good ol' cabbage rolls. Leaf lettuce, sui choy (Napa cabbage), savoy cabbage and even ordinary cabbage can be used in this recipe. As for fish, I've used cod, lingcod and snapper to good effect. Any mild white fish will work—freshness is the key. Fresh shiitakes are preferred, but rehydrated dried Chinese mushrooms are just fine. Careful with the chilies! Add half the volume, finish the sauce, then add more to taste.

¾ lb	halibut fillet	375 g
½ tsp	salt	2 mL

Marinade:

2 tsp	minced ginger	10 mL
1 tsp	sesame oil	5 mL
1 tbsp	dry sherry	15 mL
1½ tsp	cornstarch	7 mL
1 tbsp	Chicken Stock (p. 3)	15 mL

Lettuce Wrap:

12	large iceberg lettuce leaves	12
2	shiitake mushrooms, cut in 6 slices each	2
2 tbsp	chopped green onions	25 mL

Sauce:

½ cup	Chicken Stock or Shrimp Stock (p. 6)	125 mL
1 or 2	small red chilies, seeded and sliced in thin threads	1 or 2
1 tsp	minced garlic	5 mL
1 tbsp	oyster sauce	15 mL
2 tsp	cornstarch	10 mL
1 tbsp	water	15 mL
2	sprigs fresh cilantro, for garnish	2

Oyster Sauce

This handy flavouring is an important element in Cantonese cooking. It's made from oysters, salt and water, with a little caramel and cornstarch added for colour and viscosity. When used sparingly it adds a subtle depth of flavour to a variety of meat, seafood and vegetable dishes. Prices will reflect the quality of the sauce. An opened bottle of oyster sauce will keep indefinitely in your refrigerator.

1. Cut halibut into 12 fingers. Season with salt, add to combined marinade ingredients and marinate for about 10 minutes.

2. Blanch lettuce leaves in boiling water until just wilted, about 45 seconds. Remove from blanching water and rinse under cold water until thoroughly cooled. Drain well, then carefully spread out each leaf, trim off thick stem parts, place on plate, cover with damp towel and set aside.

3. Return blanching water to medium-high heat and place steamer over water.

4. To make fish rolls: place halibut finger, mushroom slice and sprinkle of green onions near base of lettuce leaf. Fold bottom of lettuce over mixture, bring sides in towards centre and continue folding into neat parcel. Place parcel open edge down on large platter that will fit into steamer. Repeat procedure for each fish roll.

5. Place finished platter in steamer, cover and steam for 4 minutes.

6. Meanwhile, in skillet, bring chicken stock to boil. Add chilies and garlic and cook for about 1 minute. Mix oyster sauce, cornstarch and water and add to boiling stock. Continue cooking for about 1 minute or until sauce is slightly thickened. Keep warm.

7. When fish rolls are cooked, transfer to warm serving plate. Pour juices into sauce and reheat sauce slightly to thicken. Pour sauce evenly over fish, garnish with cilantro and serve immediately.

Serves 4

Each serving provides:		
	Calories	108
g	Carbohydrates	5
g	Protein	14
g	Fat	3
g	Saturated Fat	tr
mg	Cholesterol	3
g	Fibre	1
mg	Sodium	335
mg	Potassium	481

Excellent: vitamin C; vitamin B-12

Good: vitamin A; vitamin D; niacin; vitamin B-6; folacin

Pan-roasted Snapper Fillets with Chinese Ratatouille

See photo, page 39

Ratatouille:

1 1/2 tsp	olive oil	7 mL
1	medium onion, chopped	1
2 tbsp	chopped ginger	25 mL
1	Chinese eggplant, diced	1
1	mo qua, peeled, seeded and diced or medium zucchini, diced	1
2 cups	chopped tomatoes	500 ml
1 tbsp	chopped garlic	15 mL
1/2 cup	Chicken Stock (p. 3) or Vegetable Stock (p. 4)	125 mL
1/4 tsp	salt	1 mL
1 tsp	sugar	5 mL
2 tbsp	chopped green onions	25 mL

Fish:

1 lb	snapper fillets, rinsed and dried	500 g
1/2 tsp	salt	2 mL
1/2 tsp	pepper	2 mL
1 tbsp	cornstarch	15 mL
1 1/2 tsp	canola oil	7 mL

Pesto

To stretch the fusion theme further, serve this with a Chinese "pesto" on the side. Combine 2 tbsp/25 mL chicken stock, 2 cloves garlic, 1/2 cup/125 mL toasted walnuts and 1/2 cup/125 mL fresh cilantro in a processor or blender and pulse to a paste. Season with a pinch of salt and pepper to taste. Serve it with this dish or with steamed or roasted chicken. This recipe has 4 g unsaturated fat per tablespoon so exercise moderation while you enjoy it.

Pesto: Serves 8

	Calories	49
g	Carbohydrates	1
g	Protein	2
g	Fat	4
g	Saturated Fat	tr
mg	Cholesterol	0
g	Fibre	tr
mg	Sodium	tr
mg	Potassium	49

1. Preheat oven to 400°F/200°C.
2. In non-stick skillet or wok, heat olive oil over medium-high heat. Add onions, ginger, eggplant and mo qua or zucchini and saute for 2 minutes.
3. Add tomatoes, garlic and stock and bring to boil. Cover and continue to cook for 5 minutes or until vegetables are tender. Season with salt and sugar. Remove from heat, stir in green onions and keep warm.
4. In small bowl, combine salt, pepper and cornstarch. Dredge fish fillets in mixture until evenly coated.
5. In a large ovenproof non-stick skillet, heat oil to medium-high. Add fish fillets and fry for 1 minute on each side or until just golden. Place pan with fish in oven and bake for 5 minutes or until fish flakes easily. Serve with ratatouille. Serve pesto on the side if desired.

Serves 4

Each serving provides:

	Calories	167
g	Carbohydrates	14
g	Protein	18
g	Fat	5
g	Saturated Fat	1
mg	Cholesterol	28
g	Fibre	4
mg	Sodium	441
mg	Potassium	809

Excellent: vitamin B-12
Good: fibre; vitamin B-6; folacin

Chinese Fish Frittata

Fish and Marinade:

½ lb	skinless white fish fillet, sliced thinly on the diagonal	250 g
¼ tsp	salt	1 mL
¼ tsp	white pepper	1 mL
2 tsp	minced garlic	10 mL
2 tbsp	chopped green onions or Chinese chives	25 mL
1 tbsp	Chinese cooking wine or dry sherry	15 mL
½ cup	flour	125 mL
3	large eggs, beaten	3
1 tbsp	canola oil	15 mL
1½ tsp	fish sauce	7 mL
2 tbsp	coarsely chopped cilantro	25 mL
1½ tsp	toasted onion flakes (p. 122, step 2)	7 mL

1. Preheat oven broiler to high and set rack about 6 inches/15 cm from heat.
2. Mix marinade ingredients, add fish and set aside for 5 minutes.
3. Sprinkle flour on a plate. Dredge each slice of fish in flour to coat evenly then dip coated slices in beaten eggs.
4. Heat oil in large ovenproof non-stick skillet over medium heat. Add fish slices and fry until half-done, about 1 minute. Fish should be just turning opaque. Pour remaining eggs over fish pieces and cook for 30 seconds.
5. Place pan under broiler and cook for about 1 minute or until eggs are set and golden on top.
6. To serve, gently loosen frittata, then turn onto platter. Brush frittata with fish sauce and sprinkle with cilantro and toasted onion flakes.

Serves 4

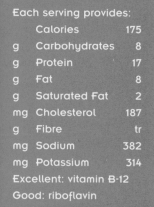

Each serving provides:

	Calories	175
g	Carbohydrates	8
g	Protein	17
g	Fat	8
g	Saturated Fat	2
mg	Cholesterol	187
g	Fibre	tr
mg	Sodium	382
mg	Potassium	314

Excellent: vitamin B-12

Good: riboflavin

Steamed Seafood Pinwheels

Here's another way to use the Fish Balls on page 25. In this recipe, use half salmon in the mixture if you want better colour. The fat content will increase slightly because salmon is a fattier fish, but you can use only egg whites for the roll if you want to compensate.

1	recipe Fish Balls (p. 25), uncooked	1
3	dried Chinese mushrooms, soaked and finely chopped	3
	vegetable oil spray	
4	large eggs, beaten	4

Sauce:

1 tbsp	fish sauce	15 mL
1 tsp	honey, or to taste	5 mL
1	small red chili, seeded and finely chopped	1
½ cup	Chicken Stock (p. 3) or Shrimp Stock (p. 6)	125 mL
1 tsp	sesame oil	5 mL
1 tsp	cornstarch	5 mL
2 tbsp	chopped cilantro leaves	25 mL

1. In large bowl, combine fish ball mixture with chopped mushrooms and mix well.
2. Heat non-stick skillet over high heat. Spray lightly with vegetable oil spray. Add 1 to 2 tbsp/15 to 25 mL beaten egg to pan and swirl to form crepe. Cook until set, turn and cook other side for 15 seconds. Repeat with remainder of eggs and stack using waxed paper to separate. Should make 6 crepes. Trim crepes into squares. Chop up trimmings finely and add to fish mixture.
3. In small bowl, combine sauce ingredients and set aside.
4. Divide fish mixture into six portions. Spread one portion of fish mixture evenly onto trimmed crepe leaving about 1 inch/2.5 cm uncovered on one side. Roll towards uncovered side to form tight roll. Place open end down on platter or steamer rack and repeat with other rolls.
5. Place in steamer and steam for 10 minutes. When done, remove and cool slightly. Slice rolls into ½-inch/1 cm slices and arrange on plate.
6. Meanwhile, heat sauce ingredients until sauce is thickened. Stir in cilantro, pour on rolls and serve.

Serves 4

Each serving (including Fish Balls) provides:

	Calories	240
g	Carbohydrates	8
g	Protein	32
g	Fat	8
g	Saturated Fat	2
mg	Cholesterol	260
g	Fibre	1
mg	Sodium	628
mg	Potassium	684

Excellent: vitamin D; vitamin C; riboflavin; vitamin B-12
Good: vitamin A; vitamin B-6; folacin; zinc

Fish in Wine Sauce

The original recipe calls for deep-frying the fish in batter first, but I've forgone that for HeartSmart reasons. If you like a bit of spice and more colour, add 1 finely chopped red chili to the sauce. For just colour, add bell peppers.

1 lb	cod, halibut or other firm white fish fillet, cut in ½-inch/1 cm slices	500 g
¼ tsp	salt	1 mL
¼ tsp	white pepper	1 mL
1½ tsp	canola oil	7 mL

Sauce:

1 tsp	minced garlic	5 mL
2 tsp	minced ginger	10 mL
2 tsp	cornstarch	10 mL
2 tbsp	cider vinegar	25 mL
¼ cup	white wine	50 mL
½ cup	Chicken Stock (p. 3) or Shrimp Stock (p. 6)	125 mL
1 tbsp	soy sauce	15 mL
4 tsp	sugar, or to taste	20 mL
1 tsp	sesame oil	5 mL
2	green onions, chopped	2

1. Rub fish with salt and pepper and set aside for 5 minutes.
2. Combine all sauce ingredients, mix well and set aside.
3. Heat non-stick skillet or wok over high heat. Add oil and heat. Add fish slices and fry until just cooked, about 1 minute on each side. Remove and set aside.
4. Add sauce mixture and bring to boil. Add green onions and cook for 1 minute, stirring constantly until sauce is thickened. Add cooked fish and gently combine. Serve immediately.

Serves 4

Each serving provides:

	Calories	168
g	Carbohydrates	7
g	Protein	23
g	Fat	4
g	Saturated Fat	tr
mg	Cholesterol	54
g	Fibre	tr
mg	Sodium	453
mg	Potassium	487

Excellent: vitamin B-12

Squid with Hot Bean Sauce

*If you like a little culinary heat, this Szechuan-style dish is sure to
please. If not, skip the chili. If you've made it and it's too spicy, add
a touch more vinegar to help tone it down.*

1 lb	cleaned squid	500 g
1 tsp	pepper	5 mL
1 tbsp	cornstarch	15 mL

Sauce:

¼ cup	Chicken Stock (p. 3) or Shrimp Stock (p. 6)	50 mL
1½ tsp	cornstarch	7 mL
1½ tsp	soy sauce	7 mL
2 tsp	sugar	10 mL
1½ tsp	Chinese black vinegar or balsamic vinegar	7 mL
2 tsp	canola oil	10 mL
½ tsp	sesame oil	2 mL
5	thin slices ginger	5
1 tbsp	minced garlic	15 mL
1	small onion, thinly sliced	1
½ tsp	five-spice powder	2 mL
1	red chili or jalapeno, seeded and finely chopped	1
1½ tsp	hot bean paste	7 mL
1	large green bell pepper, coarsely diced	1
1	small red or yellow bell pepper, coarsely diced	1
1 tbsp	dry sherry	15 mL

1. Score squid lightly with sharp knife, making diagonal crisscross pattern. Be careful not to cut completely through meat. Then cut into 2-inch/5 cm pieces. Combine squid with pepper and cornstarch and let sit for 5 minutes.

2. Combine sauce ingredients and set aside.

3. Heat oil in non-stick skillet or wok over high heat. Add squid and stir-fry for 30 seconds to 1 minute, or until squid pieces just turn opaque and begin to curl. Remove squid, sprinkle with sesame oil and set aside.

4. Add ginger, garlic, onion, five-spice, chili and hot bean paste to same pan and stir-fry for 30 seconds.

5. Add sweet peppers and sherry, stir and cook for 1 minute. Add sauce mixture and stir for 1 minute or until sauce is thickened.

6. Return cooked squid to pan, toss to mix and serve immediately.

Serves 4

Each serving provides:	
Calories	194
g Carbohydrates	13
g Protein	21
g Fat	6
g Saturated Fat	tr
mg Cholesterol	tr
g Fibre	2
mg Sodium	262
mg Potassium	174

Excellent: vitamin A;
vitamin C
Good: iron

Steamed Oysters with Garlic Topping

Here's a simple way to capture the freshness of oysters or other shell-fish. The Chinese love large oysters. If you use smaller ones, you may wish to increase their number and shorten the cooking time.

| 8 | large oysters, shucked and left on halfshell (retain oyster liquor in shells) | 8 |

Topping:

2 tsp	canola oil	10 mL
1/4 cup	finely chopped garlic	50 mL
2 tbsp	brandy	25 mL
2 tbsp	thinly sliced green onion	25 mL

1. Arrange oysters in halfshells on heat-resistant plate ready for steamer.
2. Heat small skillet over medium heat. Add oil, then add garlic and cook until pale golden, about 30 seconds, stirring constantly.
3. Add brandy and ignite, shaking pan to mix; cook until alcohol is burned off, about 15 seconds.
4. Spoon topping over each oyster. Top with green onion.
5. Place plate of oysters in steamer. Cover and steam for 5 minutes. Serve immediately.

Serves 4

Oysters

Choose oysters that are hefty and firmly closed. To shuck, protect one hand with a thick towel and hold oyster firmly. Wriggle the oyster knife into the hinge of the oyster (the small end) until the knife point is well lodged. Twist the oyster knife lightly while applying inward pressure until you hear a pop and feel the shell loosen. Pry the shell open and cut the adductor muscle (the muscle that looks like a small scallop).

Each serving provides:

	Calories	117
g	Carbohydrates	8
g	Protein	10
g	Fat	5
g	Saturated Fat	1
mg	Cholesterol	50
g	Fibre	tr
mg	Sodium	107
mg	Potassium	213

Excellent: zinc; vitamin D; iron; vitamin B-12
Good: riboflavin

Stir-fried Mussels with Chinese Chives and Bean Sprouts

Choose large mussels for this savoury stir-fry. They should be heavy and firmly closed: discard open ones before cooking. Frozen New Zealand green mussels are a good choice here. They are often par-cooked so you can skip the initial steaming.

1 cup	white wine	250 mL
3	slices ginger	3
1	large green onion, smashed and cut in quarters	1
2 lb	mussels in shell, scrubbed and debearded	1 kg
2 tsp	cornstarch	10 mL
1 tbsp	hot bean paste	15 mL
2 tsp	minced garlic	10 mL
1 tbsp	chopped shallots	15 mL
4	large dried Chinese mushrooms, soaked and thinly sliced	4
1	bunch flowering chives, cut in 2-inch/5 cm lengths	1
1	red bell pepper, seeded, thinly sliced	1
4 cups	bean sprouts	1 L

1. In large pot, bring white wine to boil. Add ginger slices, green onion and mussels. Cover and simmer for about 2 minutes or until mussels are open. Shake pot occasionally to help mussels open and ensure even cooking. Be careful not to overcook.

2. Strain broth from mussels into bowl and cool. Remove mussel meat from shells and discard shells. Return mussels to cooled broth and set aside. In small bowl, combine cornstarch with ¼ cup/50 mL of cooled broth and set aside.

3. Heat non-stick skillet or wok over medium-high heat. Add bean paste, garlic and shallots and stir-fry for 30 seconds or until fragrant. Add mushrooms, chives and bell peppers and stir-fry for 1 minute.

4. Drain mussels, add to vegetable mixture and stir. Add cornstarch mixture and stir for 1 minute or until vegetables begin to soften and liquid is mostly absorbed.

5. Add bean sprouts, toss together and cook for 1 minute until heated through. Serve immediately.

Serves 4

Chinese Chives
Garlic chives, Chinese flowering chives, gau choy fa

This cousin of the western chive has a garlicky flavour—hence the confusing nickname shared with the leaves of the garlic plant. Chinese chives have flat, hollow leaves. Flowering chives are the tubular flowering stalks topped with pointed white flower buds. They are used as garnish or enjoyed in stir-fried dishes as a vegetable.

Each serving provides:

	Calories	146
g	Carbohydrates	14
g	Protein	11
g	Fat	5
g	Saturated Fat	1
mg	Cholesterol	16
g	Fibre	3
mg	Sodium	429
mg	Potassium	473

Excellent: iron; vitamin C; folacin; vitamin B-12

Good: vitamin A; vitamin D; fibre; thiamine; riboflavin; zinc

Spicy Garlic Prawns

It was my birthday and my first visit to one of the famous floating restaurants in Aberdeen harbour in Hong Kong. I had the privilege of making the first pick for dinner and I knew what I wanted. I remember stepping gingerly across the decks of the sampans tied up alongside and peering into the large wooden barrels that served as makeshift holding tanks for the live fish and shellfish. Lit by a kerosene lamp, the six-inch-long prawns were a captivating sight. In taste, they were simply splendid—firm, succulent and sweet. All these years later, the sight of live prawns still sets my taste buds tingling.

If you aren't squeamish, try this recipe with live prawns; they're well worth the extra cost. Of course, good-quality frozen prawns in the shell are also great. Cooked in the shell, prawns keep their juices and add some excitement to your table.

Sauce:

¼ tsp	salt	1 mL
1 tsp	soy sauce	5 mL
3 tbsp	water	45 mL
2 tbsp	dry sherry	25 mL
1 lb	tiger prawns	500 g
1 tbsp	canola oil	15 mL
6	cloves garlic, chopped fine	6
1 tsp	hot red pepper flakes	5 mL

1. Combine sauce ingredients and set aside.
2. Trim legs and feelers off prawns with scissors. If you are using prawns with heads on, trim off part of the head just behind the eyes. With sharp knife, score backs of prawns through shell and remove vein. Rinse with cold water and pat dry.
3. Heat wok or skillet over high heat, add oil and heat until oil starts to smoke lightly. Add garlic and pepper flakes and brown lightly. Add prawns and cook for about 2 minutes, tossing to cook evenly.
4. Pour in sauce mixture. Stir well and cook until prawns turn pink and completely opaque, about 3 minutes. Serve immediately. Reserve shells for Shrimp Stock (p. 6).

Serves 4

Each serving provides:

	Calories	154
g	Carbohydrates	3
g	Protein	23
g	Fat	4
g	Saturated Fat	tr
mg	Cholesterol	170
g	Fibre	tr
mg	Sodium	220
mg	Potassium	33

Good: iron

Tea-smoked Seafood

See photo, page 40

Tea smoking comes from Szechuan and Hunan in China's western region, where it is mostly used for ducks and poultry. I have combined the method with a marinade from an eastern Chinese fish dish and a Cantonese dip for this Chinese regional fusion dish.

Seafood and Marinade:

2	green onions, cut in quarters	2
5	slices ginger	5
3 tbsp	soy sauce	45 mL
1 tbsp	dry sherry	15 mL
2 tsp	sugar	10 mL
1/2 tsp	five-spice powder	2 mL
1 lb	seafood (peeled and deveined prawns, scallops, fish fillet chunks)	500 g

Dip:

1/3 cup	plain skim milk yogurt	75 mL
1/3 cup	1% buttermilk	75 mL
3/4 cup	finely diced honeydew and cantaloupe	175 mL

Tea Smoke Mixture:

1/2 cup	raw white rice	125 mL
1/2 cup	black tea leaves	125 mL
1/2 cup	white sugar	125 mL

1. Crush green onions and ginger, place in deep dish. Add remainder of marinade ingredients and seafood and marinate for about 20 minutes. Thread seafood on bamboo skewers if desired for easy handling.

2. Combine all dip ingredients in small bowl.

3. To prepare for tea smoke, use aluminum foil to line large pan that has a tight-fitting lid. Spread mixed tea smoke materials evenly in pan. Oil cake or round rack. Place rack above mixture in pan and cover.

4. Increase heat to medium-high and allow smoker to heat up, about 4 minutes. (Turn on ventilation fan in your house if you are doing this indoors. See sidebar for directions on tea smoking on the barbecue.)

5. When material is smoking, place seafood on rack; cover and allow to cook and smoke, about 3 minutes per side. Serve warm or cold with dip.

Serves 6

Tea Smoking

Tea smoking can easily be done on a barbecue if you want to keep your kitchen smoke free. Put the pan with the tea mixture directly on the coals and the food on the barbecue rack.

Each serving provides:

	Calories	144
g	Carbohydrates	7
g	Protein	25
g	Fat	1
g	Saturated Fat	tr
mg	Cholesterol	170
g	Fibre	tr
mg	Sodium	542
mg	Potassium	139

Good: iron

See Qua

Angled luffa, sing qua
Distinguished by the sharp ridges on its skin, this squash is dull green and looks like a long English cucumber crossed with an okra. When cooked, it's sweet and crunchy. To peel see qua, use a potato peeler and remove the ridges, leaving part of the skin on. This will give the pieces a pretty green-and-white zebra pattern when cut. Medium-sized ones are 1–1½ feet/ 30–45 cm long. They should be firm, plump, hefty and free of blemishes.

Each serving provides:

	Calories	193
g	Carbohydrates	10
g	Protein	20
g	Fat	8
g	Saturated Fat	1
mg	Cholesterol	120
g	Fibre	2
mg	Sodium	139
mg	Potassium	382

Good: folacin; iron

Prawns with Cashews and See Qua

Chicken with cashews, the long-time favourite in North American Chinese restaurants, spawned this adaptation. It offers you a chance to try a new vegetable, see qua, also called sing qua (the word "sing" in Cantonese means victory). If you can't get see qua, substitute with long English cucumbers, but shorten the cooking time of the vegetables to 1 to 2 minutes.

1 tbsp	canola oil	15 mL
1	medium onion, sliced	1
3	slices ginger	3
¾ lb	medium-to-large prawns, shelled, deveined	375 g
1 cup	Quick Thickened Stock (chicken or shrimp) (p. 2)	250 mL
1 tbsp	dry sherry	15 mL
1	see qua, peeled, or long English cucumber, skin on, halved lengthwise and cut in thick chunks	1
¼ tsp	salt	1 mL
¼ cup	unsalted whole cashews, roasted	50 mL
¼ tsp	white pepper	1 mL

1. Heat oil in non-stick skillet or wok over high heat. Add onions and ginger and stir-fry for 30 seconds. Add prawns and stir-fry for 1 minute or until prawns are just turning opaque. Remove and set aside.
2. Add thickened stock and sherry to pan and bring to boil. If using see qua, add now. Add salt, cover and braise for 2 minutes. Uncover and cook until liquid is reduced by half. If using English cucumber, braise for 1 minute and remove while sauce reduces. Return to pan with prawn mixture.
3. Add prawn-and-onion mixture and cashews; stir to combine until warmed. Season with white pepper to taste. Serve immediately.

Serves 4

Spicy Beef with Baby Bok Choy, pages 86-87 >

Pan-fried Scallops with Pine Nuts

My love for scallops knows no bounds—especially the large eastern scallops with the orange roe attached. My neighbourhood Chinese restaurant serves this with shrimp sauce on the side to jazz it up. We chose to go the HeartSmart way with lemon juice.

1 tbsp	canola oil	15 mL
3 tbsp	pine nuts	45 mL
½ lb	large bay scallops	250 g
6	slices ginger	6
3	cloves garlic, smashed	3
1	carrot, thinly sliced	1
½ lb	snow peas, washed and trimmed	250 g
2 tbsp	dry sherry	25 mL
¼ cup	Chicken Stock (p. 3) or Vegetable Stock (p. 4), divided	50 mL
2 tsp	fish sauce	10 mL
1½ tsp	cornstarch	7 mL
1 tbsp	lemon juice	15 mL

1. In non-stick skillet or wok, heat oil over medium-high heat. Fry pine nuts briefly in oil until just golden but not brown, stirring constantly. Remove nuts with slotted spoon and dry on paper towel. (Nuts will burn quickly; they continue to cook after being removed from heat.)
2. Turn heat to high and add scallops to pan. Sear scallops for about 30 seconds on each side, or until scallops turn opaque and lightly golden. Remove and set aside.
3. Reduce heat to medium-high. Add ginger, garlic, carrots and snow peas to same pan and stir for 1 minute. Add sherry and 2 tbsp/25 mL stock, cover and cook for 1 minute.
4. Combine remaining chicken stock, fish sauce and cornstarch and mix well.
5. Add scallops and pine nuts and stir for 30 seconds or until sauce thickens. Sprinkle with lemon juice and mix. Serve immediately.

Serves 4

Pine Nuts

Most people think pine nuts, the seeds of the stone pine, are Italian, but the Chinese have also used them for centuries. Like other seeds, they are a festival food signifying prosperity in progeny—having a lot of children—which, while not necessarily desirable in modern China, has not detracted from their popularity. Pine nuts are high in fat (61%, mostly mono- and polyunsaturated), but their intense flavour means you can use them sparingly.

Each serving provides:

	Calories	188
g	Carbohydrates	9
g	Protein	12
g	Fat	12
g	Saturated Fat	2
mg	Cholesterol	20
g	Fibre	3
mg	Sodium	477
mg	Potassium	400

Excellent: vitamin A; vitamin B-12
Good: thiamine; vitamin E; fibre

< *Miso Pork with Water Chestnuts and Snow Peas,* page 99

Lemon Grass

This cream-coloured grass from Southeast Asia has a complex lemony flavour and fragrance. Fresh or frozen is best. Use only the fleshy bulb part at the base; save the rest to perfume a fish stock. Lemon juice and zest will make an adequate substitute.

Kaffir Lime Leaves

Kaffir leaves are available fresh, frozen or dried. Dried leaves need to be rehydrated before use. No substitute can truly compare, but lime zest and juice can be used if necessary.

Each serving provides:

	Calories	234
g	Carbohydrates	14
g	Protein	19
g	Fat	11
g	Saturated Fat	9
mg	Cholesterol	59
g	Fibre	3
mg	Sodium	791
mg	Potassium	426

Excellent: vitamin B-12

Good: fibre; calcium; vitamin C

Baked Twin Lobsters in Coconut Curry

I don't know anyone who doesn't like lobster, so here's a special occasion dish inspired by the fragrances of Thailand.

2	medium lobsters, in shell	2
1 cup	canned coconut milk, skimmed of fat	250 mL
1 stalk	lemon grass, thinly sliced or 2 tsp/10 mL lemon juice	1
5	kaffir lime leaves, thinly sliced or 2 tsp/10 mL lime zest	5
2 to 3 tsp	curry powder	10 to 15 mL
2 tbsp	finely chopped onions	25 mL
1 tsp	minced garlic	5 mL
½ cup	breadcrumbs	125 mL

Sauce:

1 tbsp	fish sauce	15 mL
1 tbsp	brandy	15 mL
3 tbsp	Chicken Stock (p. 3) or Shrimp Stock (p. 6)	45 mL
2 tsp	cornstarch	10 mL

Garnish:

5 or 6	fresh mint leaves, thinly sliced	5 or 6
1	red chili, thinly sliced	1

1. Split lobsters lengthwise and crack claws. If desired, slice lobster-tail meat into bite-sized pieces and return to shell. Place on baking sheet open side up and set aside. Heat oven to 400°F/200°C.
2. In small skillet, bring coconut milk to boil. Add lemon grass, lime leaves and curry powder. Reduce heat, cover and simmer for 15 minutes. Remove from heat and strain. Discard solids.
3. Return sauce to pan over medium heat. Add onions and garlic and cook for 3 minutes or until soft.
4. Combine sauce ingredients. Add to skillet and bring to boil. Continue to cook until sauce is slightly thickened.
5. Carefully pour sauce onto lobster halves to cover. Sprinkle breadcrumbs over sauce. Place in oven and bake for 10 to 12 minutes or until lobster flesh is firm and white.
6. Transfer to serving platter. Sprinkle mint leaves and chili slices on lobster and serve.

Serves 6

Broccoli with Crab and Tofu Sauce

Broccoli is a staple in my house and I'm always looking for a way to zip it up for my kids. This saucy dish succeeded in making them eat tofu as well! They love it spooned onto steamed rice. Recently I had a version of it served with fresh straw mushrooms and B.C. cultivated asparagus.

Sauce:

2 tbsp	cornstarch	25 mL
1 tbsp	soy sauce	15 mL
¼ tsp	seasoning salt	1 mL
½ tsp	white pepper	2 mL
2 tbsp	water or Chicken Stock (p. 3)	25 mL
1 tsp	sesame oil	5 mL
¾ cup	Chicken Stock	175 mL
1½ lb	broccoli florets	750 g
1 tbsp	canola oil	15 mL
2 tsp	minced ginger	10 mL
1½ cups	fresh crabmeat, Dungeness if possible	375 mL
1½ cups	Chicken Stock or Chinese-style Vegetable Stock (p. 5)	375 mL
1	10-oz/300 g package soft tofu, cut in tiny cubes	1
1	egg white, lightly beaten	1
2 tbsp	chopped green onions	25 mL

1. Combine sauce ingredients and set aside.

2. In large non-stick skillet, bring ¾ cup/175 mL chicken stock to boil over medium-high heat. Add broccoli and seasoning salt and stir for 30 seconds until well coated. Cover and cook for 2 minutes or until broccoli is tender-crisp. Drain, arrange on serving plate and keep warm.

3. Heat oil in non-stick skillet over medium-high heat. Add ginger and crabmeat and stir for 15 seconds.

4. Add the 1½ cups/375 mL chicken stock and bring to boil. Add tofu and cook for 1 minute, stirring gently to mix.

5. Add sauce mixture, stir and cook until sauce is slightly thickened. Add egg white and stir gently to form swirls, about 30 seconds. Add green onions and mix. Pour sauce over broccoli and serve.

Serves 6

Each serving provides:

	Calories	136
g	Carbohydrates	10
g	Protein	14
g	Fat	6
g	Saturated Fat	1
mg	Cholesterol	22
g	Fibre	4
mg	Sodium	415
mg	Potassium	557

Excellent: vitamin A; vitamin E; vitamin C; folacin; vitamin B-12; iron; Good: riboflavin; niacin; vitamin B-6

Stir-fried Clams with Black Beans

This Cantonese dish is so popular in North America that it has become the definitive Chinese food here. It has also found its way onto the menus of pasta bars and fusion restaurants in the past decade. One Chinatown restaurant in Vancouver, now defunct, achieved national fame with it and served it to no less than three prime ministers as well as countless other celebrities.

Fermented Black Beans
Tou shih

These predate soy sauce because they're easy to produce and portable. Before use they should be rinsed and dried on paper towels. The classic black bean sauce contains garlic, ginger, fermented black beans, wine and sometimes, for meat dishes, a bit of dried tangerine peel.

1 tbsp	fermented black beans	15 mL
Sauce:		
2 tbsp	Chicken Stock (p. 3)	25 mL
2 tsp	cornstarch	10 mL
1 tsp	soy sauce	5 mL
1 1/2 tsp	oyster sauce	7 mL
1 1/2 tsp	canola oil	7 mL
1	shallot, finely chopped	1
2 tsp	minced ginger	10 mL
1 tsp	minced garlic	5 mL
1	small red chili, seeded and chopped (optional)	1
2 lb	clams or mussels, scrubbed clean	1 kg
1/2 cup	Chicken Stock or Vegetable Stock (p. 4)	125 mL
2 tbsp	dry sherry	25 mL
2 tbsp	chopped green onions	25 mL

1. Rinse and soak fermented black beans in cold water for 30 minutes, pat dry with paper towel and mash.
2. Combine sauce ingredients and set aside.
3. In large skillet or wok, heat oil over high heat. Add black beans, shallot, ginger, garlic and chili (if desired) and stir-fry for 30 seconds.
4. Add clams and stir to mix for 1 minute. Add stock and sherry and bring to boil. Cover and allow to steam for 3 minutes or until clamshells open. Shake pan occasionally to ensure even cooking.
5. Add sauce mixture and stir until sauce is thickened, about 1 minute. Add green onions, stir to mix well and serve.

Serves 4

Each serving provides:

	Calories	113
g	Carbohydrates	7
g	Protein	13
g	Fat	3
g	Saturated Fat	tr
mg	Cholesterol	16
g	Fibre	tr
mg	Sodium	360
mg	Potassium	405

Excellent: vitamin C; vitamin B-12; iron
Good: vitamin A; zinc

Chiu Chow Lemon Duck Soup

This soup takes me back to the gentler days when a soup pot would be left simmering happily all day long until dinner. The meat, mixed with vegetables and flavourings, can be returned to the soup or served on the side. Whole-wheat pita bread makes a fibre-rich accompaniment.

1	3-lb/1.5 kg duck	1
½	lemon	½
20	whole black peppercorns	20
5	cloves	5
12 cups	cold water	3 L

Garnish:

1 tsp	soy sauce	5 mL
1 tsp	sesame oil	5 mL
1 tsp	Vietnamese chili sauce	5 mL
2 tbsp	Quick Thickened Stock (p. 2)	25 mL
¼ tsp	minced garlic	1 mL
1 cup	carrot, cut in matchsticks	250 mL
1 cup	cucumber, cut in matchsticks	250 mL

1. Trim duck of all fat and skin, cut into quarters and rinse well under cold running water. If you have time, blanch duck pieces in boiling water for about 2 minutes and drain for clearer broth.
2. Tie lemon, peppercorns and cloves into cheesecloth pouch to make bouquet garni.
3. Add cold water, duck and bouquet garni to heavy Dutch oven and bring to slow boil over medium heat, uncovered. Skim off foam periodically. Reduce heat, cover and cook soup at low simmer for 2 to 2½ hours or until meat is very tender and comes off bones easily.
4. Remove duck and bouquet garni, discard bones and slice duck meat. Skim fat off soup. For easiest removal, chill overnight and scrape off solid fat the next day.
5. In large bowl, combine soy sauce, sesame oil, chili sauce, thickened stock and garlic and mix well. Add duck meat and vegetables and toss well. Divide into individual bowls, pour soup over and serve. Or serve soup alone, garnished with chopped green onions and mint leaves, with meat and vegetables served separately.

Serves 8

Duck Fat

Duck is a very fatty bird, so take care to remove all the visible fat before cooking. The leanest duck soup is made a day ahead of serving so you can refrigerate it and remove the solidified fat from the broth.

Each serving provides:

	Calories	210
g	Carbohydrates	7
g	Protein	21
g	Fat	11
g	Saturated Fat	4
mg	Cholesterol	76
g	Fibre	3
mg	Sodium	116
mg	Potassium	332

Excellent: vitamin A; riboflavin; zinc
Good: fibre; vitamin E; thiamine; niacin; vitamin B-12; iron

Chopped Chicken in Lettuce Wrap

The original recipe is a New Year specialty calling for game birds and dried oysters. Lettuce or sung choy *is used because the word "sung" also means being alive and signifies longevity. The oysters are* ho shih, *which sounds the same as the phrase "good things." Eating this dish will lead to a good life in the year to come. Try it with your Christmas turkey leftovers.*

4	dried Chinese mushrooms, soaked and finely diced	4
1	2-oz/60 g pkg cellophane noodles, soaked and coarsely chopped	1

Chicken and Marinade:

1 lb	boneless, skinless chicken breast, cut in small dice	500 g
½ tsp	pepper	2 mL
1 tbsp	dry sherry	15 mL
1½ tsp	cornstarch	7 mL
1 tbsp	canola oil	15 mL
1	small onion, diced	1
1 cup	diced carrot	250 mL
1 cup	diced broccoli stems	250 mL
8	water chestnuts, peeled and diced	8
½ cup	Quick Thickened Stock (p. 2)	125 mL
1 tsp	soy sauce	5 mL
1 tbsp	hoisin sauce	15 mL
1 tsp	sesame oil	5 mL
2 tbsp	chopped cilantro	25 mL
12	leaves iceberg lettuce	12

1. As mushrooms and noodles soak, combine chicken and marinade ingredients and marinate for 10 minutes.
2. Heat oil in wok over high heat. Add onions and chicken and stir-fry for 1 minute.
3. Reduce heat to medium-high, add diced mushrooms, carrots and broccoli stems and stir-fry for 2 minutes.
4. Add water chestnuts, chopped noodles, thickened stock, soy sauce, hoisin sauce and sesame oil and continue cooking for 2 minutes or until vegetables are just soft and liquid is absorbed. Remove from heat and add chopped cilantro.
5. Serve chicken on large platter with raw lettuce leaves on the side so diners can make rolls themselves.

Serves 6

Chicken Hint

To make chicken easier to dice or slice, place it in freezer for about ½ hour or until it's just beginning to freeze, then cut according to recipe instructions. This works for all other meats too.

Each serving provides:
	Calories	191
g	Carbohydrates	19
g	Protein	17
g	Fat	5
g	Saturated Fat	1
mg	Cholesterol	42
g	Fibre	2
mg	Sodium	229
mg	Potassium	440

Excellent: vitamin A; niacin
Good: vitamin C; folacin;
vitamin D; vitamin B-6

Warm Chicken, Watercress and Pomelo Salad

Pomelo
Chinese grapefruit

When buying pomelos, look for fruits that are heavy and rich in aroma. A smooth, well-filled rind generally indicates freshness, but some people think the fruit mellows and becomes richer and juicier when stored for a short time. The individual vesicles of the pomelo are large and do not burst easily, so they can be separated into strands for exciting presentations.

The pomelo was popular for centuries in its native Indochina before it acquired its other name, shaddock, in honour of Captain Shaddock, who introduced it to the West Indies in the mid-seventeenth century. According to most sources, the pomelo was crossed with the sweet orange to beget the grapefruit, which launched its successful career as a commercial fruit in the 1880s in Florida.

Dressing:

2 tbsp	lime juice	25 mL
4 tsp	fish sauce	20 mL
1 tbsp	brown sugar	15 mL
1/4 cup	Chicken Stock (p. 3) or Chinese-style Vegetable Stock (p. 5)	50 mL
2	garlic cloves, crushed	2
1	small red chili, seeded and sliced	1
1	stem lemon grass, fleshy bulb only, sliced thinly on the diagonal	1
1	bunch watercress, washed and trimmed	1
1	pomelo or 2 grapefruits, peeled and sectioned	1
1 lb	skinless, boneless chicken breast	500 g
1 1/2 tsp	olive oil	7 mL

1. Combine dressing ingredients and set aside.
2. Place watercress in centre of each serving plate. Arrange pomelo sections around watercress.
3. Slice chicken into strips. In non-stick skillet, heat oil over medium heat. Add chicken strips and saute until golden, about 2 minutes.
4. Add dressing mixture and bring to boil for 1 minute.
5. Divide and pour hot chicken mixture onto watercress on each plate and serve.

Serves 4

Each serving provides:

	Calories	214
g	Carbohydrates	17
g	Protein	26
g	Fat	5
g	Saturated Fat	1
mg	Cholesterol	67
g	Fibre	3
mg	Sodium	579
mg	Potassium	585

Excellent: vitamin C; niacin; vitamin B-12
Good: fibre; vitamin B-6

Stir-fried Chicken with Yard-long Beans

A simple but tasty recipe for chicken. I like it with asparagus when it's in season. Ordinary green beans, bok choy, broccoli, celery—nearly any green vegetable works well here.

Chicken and Marinade:

1 lb	boneless, skinless chicken breast, thinly sliced	500 g
1 tbsp	soy sauce	15 mL
1 tbsp	cornstarch	15 mL
1 tbsp	water	15 mL
1 tbsp	dry sherry	15 mL
1 tbsp	canola oil	15 mL
6	thick slices ginger	6
1	large shallot, finely chopped	1
½ cup	Quick Thickened Stock (chicken or rich pork) (p. 2)	125 mL
1 lb	yard-long beans or asparagus, washed, trimmed, cut in 2-inch/5 cm segments	500 g
2 tsp	minced garlic	10 mL
1 tbsp	fish sauce	15 mL
¼ tsp	sugar	1 mL
1 tsp	sesame oil	5 mL
1 tsp	white pepper, or to taste	5 mL

1. Combine chicken with marinade ingredients, and set aside for at least 30 minutes or overnight.

2. Heat non-stick skillet or wok over medium-high heat. Add oil and heat until just smoking. Add ginger and shallots and fry until fragrant, about 30 seconds. Add chicken and stir-fry evenly for about 2 minutes or until chicken begins to turn opaque. Remove chicken and set aside.

3. Add thickened stock to pan and bring to boil. Add yard-long beans and garlic and stir-fry for 1 minute. Add fish sauce and sugar and cover to cook for 2 minutes or until vegetables are just tender. Uncover, add sesame oil and toss to mix.

4. Return chicken to pan and continue cooking until liquid is mostly absorbed. Season with white pepper. Serve immediately.

Serves 4

Yard-long Beans
Asparagus beans, dow gok

One common name comes from their unusual length of up to 18 inches/45 cm. When cooked they turn bright green and taste a bit like asparagus, a fact responsible for their other common name. Look for beans that are plump and firm.

Each serving provides:

	Calories	229
g	Carbohydrates	14
g	Protein	27
g	Fat	7
g	Saturated Fat	1
mg	Cholesterol	65
g	Fibre	4
mg	Sodium	661
mg	Potassium	514

Excellent: niacin; vitamin B-6; folacin; vitamin B-12
Good: iron; fibre; vitamin C

Stir-fried Chicken with Mango

An all-around hit with our tasters, this colourful dish made the cover. It's a good example of new-style Chinese cooking which incorporates different fresh fruits as flavourings. Peaches, lychees and other soft fruits are now used in different dishes and can be used here.

Chicken and Marinade:

¾ lb	boneless, skinless chicken breast, sliced	375 g
1½ tsp	soy sauce	7 mL
¼ tsp	salt	1 mL
pinch	white pepper	pinch
1 tsp	cornstarch	5 mL

Sauce:

2 tsp	cider vinegar	10 mL
1½ tsp	ketchup	7 mL
1½ tsp	sugar	7 mL
2 tbsp	water	25 mL

1	star anise	1
1 tbsp	canola oil	15 mL
½	medium green bell pepper, sliced	½
½	medium red bell pepper, sliced	½
1 tbsp	grated ginger	15 mL
1 tsp	garlic	5 mL
1	large shallot, chopped	1
2	large mangoes, peeled, pitted, thinly sliced	2
16	pieces Candied Pecans with Sesame (p. 12) or toasted pecan halves	16
2	sprigs cilantro	2

1. Combine chicken and marinade ingredients and marinate for 30 minutes.
2. Combine sauce ingredients and set aside.
3. Break off radial pieces of star anise and discard woody centre. Gently press with knife to crack lightly.
4. In non-stick skillet or wok, heat oil and star anise over high heat. Add chicken and stir-fry for 3 minutes or until chicken just turns opaque. Add peppers, ginger, garlic and shallots and stir-fry for 1 minute.
5. Add sauce ingredients and stir to mix until sauce is slightly thickened, about 1 minute. Add mangoes and mix gently for 1 minute until heated through.
6. Garnish with pecans and cilantro and serve.

Serves 4

Mango

Among Asians it's known as the Queen of Fruits. Choose mangoes that are hefty, free of skin blemishes and firm but not hard. Depending on the variety, they may be yellow, red or green when ripe. Firmer, slightly underripe mangoes are great for cooking. Cut the mango along the flatter sides of the oval (the cross-section) about ½ inch/ 1 cm from the centre line. If you hit the flat pit, cut around it. Peel.

Each serving (not including Candied Pecans) provides:

	Calories	269
g	Carbohydrates	26
g	Protein	21
g	Fat	10
g	Saturated Fat	1
mg	Cholesterol	50
g	Fibre	4
mg	Sodium	330
mg	Potassium	420

Excellent: vitamin A; vitamin C; niacin

Good: fibre; vitamin E; vitamin B-6; folacin

Grilled Quails with Orange

I have a small kitchen at home, so my barbecue is a godsend. I can marinate this dish overnight, cook the quails outside and have a bit of elbow room in the kitchen for preparing other dishes. Serve one bird as an appetizer or two as a main course with vegetables and rice.

8	quails	8

Marinade:

1 tbsp	grated ginger	15 mL
2	green onions, finely chopped	2
3	cloves garlic, peeled and minced	3
3 tbsp	soy sauce	45 mL
2 tsp	grated orange zest	10 mL
2 tbsp	orange juice concentrate	25 mL
2 tbsp	sake or white wine	25 mL
½ tsp	five-spice powder	2 mL
1 tsp	hot red pepper flakes	5 mL
2 tbsp	honey or brown sugar	25 mL
1	orange, sliced, for garnish	1

1. Butterfly each quail by splitting along backbone. Remove backbone and neck. Place each quail bone-side down and press on skin side to flatten.
2. In small saucepan over low heat, combine all marinade ingredients and stir until honey or brown sugar is melted.
3. Place quails and marinade in large self-sealing or freezer bag. Squeeze to remove all air and seal. Through bag, rub marinade thoroughly onto quails and refrigerate for 2 hours or overnight.
4. Heat barbecue with oiled rack to medium-high heat. Remove quails from marinade and reserve marinade for basting.
5. Barbecue quails skin-side down first for about 3 to 4 minutes on each side or until golden brown. Baste and turn as necessary to avoid burning. Serve with Chinese Coleslaw (p. 122) or over a bed of crisp shredded lettuce garnished with sliced oranges.

Serves 8 as appetizer

Quails

Because quail is quite a lean bird, you may eat some of the skin, but remove any fatty parts before eating.

Each serving provides:

	Calories	242
g	Carbohydrates	8
g	Protein	22
g	Fat	13
g	Saturated Fat	4
mg	Cholesterol	83
g	Fibre	tr
mg	Sodium	445
mg	Potassium	301

Excellent: niacin; vitamin B-6; iron

Good: thiamine; riboflavin; vitamin B-12

Hot and Sour Oven-fried Turkey with Candied Garlic Sauce

The technique is simple yet it manages to simulate the texture of deep-frying.

Meat Coating Mix:

½ cup	finely crushed cornflakes	125 mL
2 tbsp	cornstarch	25 mL
½ tsp	pepper	2 mL
2 tsp	paprika	10 mL
1 lb	boneless skinless turkey meat	500 g
1	egg white, lightly beaten	1
	vegetable oil spray	

Sauce:

4	cloves garlic, sliced lengthwise	4
5 tbsp	white sugar	90 mL
½ cup	white wine vinegar	125 mL
½ tsp	hot red pepper flakes	2 mL
¼ cup	finely sliced red bell pepper	50 mL

1. Preheat oven to 400°F/200°C.
2. Combine coating mix in plastic bag and set aside.
3. Cut turkey into ½-inch/1 cm cubes. Stir turkey into egg whites. Toss with coating mix in plastic bag.
4. Lightly coat baking sheet with vegetable oil spray. Arrange turkey on sheet and bake for 20 minutes. Remove turkey from oven and let stand for 5 minutes.
5. Meanwhile, in medium saucepan, combine sauce ingredients, bring to boil and continue to cook until sauce is reduced and turned light brown. Toss turkey in finished sauce.
6. Add sliced red bell pepper, cover and heat over medium heat for 1 minute. Transfer to platter and serve.

Serves 4

Each serving provides:

	Calories	355
g	Carbohydrates	39
g	Protein	36
g	Fat	6
g	Saturated Fat	2
mg	Cholesterol	86
g	Fibre	1
mg	Sodium	240
mg	Potassium	461

Good: riboflavin; niacin; vitamin B-6; vitamin B-12; iron

Curried Chicken and Roasted Root Vegetable Stew

½ lb	potatoes, peeled	250 g
½ lb	yams, peeled	250 g
½ lb	taro root or parsnips, peeled	250 g
1 tbsp	olive oil	15 mL
½ tsp	pepper	5 mL

Sauce:

1½ cups	Veal Demi-glace (p. 7) or Chicken Stock (p. 3)	375 mL
1 tbsp	curry powder	15 mL
½ tsp	five-spice powder	2 mL
1½ tsp	soy sauce	7 mL
1½ tsp	oyster sauce	7 mL

¾ lb	skinless, boneless chicken, cut in 1-inch/2.5 cm pieces	375 g
¼ tsp	salt	1 mL
¼ cup	flour	50 mL
1½ tsp	canola oil	7 mL
3	slices ginger	3
1	onion, sliced	1
2	cloves garlic, peeled and smashed	2
2	green onions, cut in eighths	2

1. Heat oven to 400°F/200°C.
2. Cut root vegetables into 1-inch/2.5 cm dice. Mix with olive oil and pepper until well coated. Spread vegetables evenly in roasting pan. Bake until just tender, turning once or twice, about 25 minutes.
3. Combine sauce ingredients and set aside.
4. Season chicken with salt and set aside.
5. Just before cooking, toss chicken in flour until evenly coated.
6. About 5 minutes before vegetables are finished roasting, heat large non-stick skillet or wok over medium-high heat. Add oil, ginger and chicken and stir-fry for 1 minute. Add onion and garlic and continue to stir-fry until all ingredients are golden brown, about 2 to 3 minutes.
7. Add sauce mixture and bring to boil. Reduce heat and cover to simmer for 5 minutes. Add roasted vegetables, mix and cover to simmer for 3 minutes, stirring occasionally.
8. Add green onions. Increase heat to medium-high and cook for 1 to 2 minutes to thicken sauce if necessary. Turn off heat, transfer to casserole dish and serve.

Serves 4

Taro

Individual tubers range from small-potato size to the size of a melon. They have coarse brown skin marked by rings, and fine root hairs. The flesh is off-white with tiny purple speckles. If you don't have taro, try using other root veggies like potatoes, parsnips and turnips, or even hard squashes.

Each serving provides:

	Calories	470
g	Carbohydrates	62
g	Protein	28
g	Fat	12
g	Saturated Fat	2
mg	Cholesterol	76
g	Fibre	7
mg	Sodium	443
mg	Potassium	1019

Excellent: fibre; vitamin A; vitamin E; niacin; vitamin B-6

Good: vitamin C; thiamine; riboflavin; calcium; iron

Kung Pao Turkey with Toasted Almonds

The original Szechuan dish calls for chicken and peanuts. Legend has it that this dish was named after a court official named Ting in the 1800s. He was a teacher to the prince (kung pao) and also helped to get rid of a powerful, corrupt official who was terrorizing the people. So his favourite dish was named "Kung Pao Chi Ting" to commemorate his achievements.

Turkey and Marinade:

1 lb	turkey breast meat, cut in 1-inch/2.5 cm cubes	500 g
2 tbsp	sherry	25 mL
1 tbsp	cornstarch	15 mL
¼ tsp	salt	1 mL
pinch	pepper	pinch

Sauce:

2 tbsp	water or Chicken Stock (p. 3)	25 mL
1 tbsp	soy sauce	15 mL
1½ tsp	hot bean paste	7 mL
2 tbsp	cider vinegar	25 mL
2 tsp	sugar	10 mL
2 tsp	cornstarch	10 mL
1 tbsp	canola oil	15 mL
2 tbsp	chopped onion	25 mL
1 tsp	chopped garlic	5 mL
2 tsp	minced ginger	10 mL
½	green bell pepper, cut in large dice	½
½	red bell pepper, cut in large dice	½
3 tbsp	Chicken Stock	45 mL
¼ cup	toasted almonds, skin on	50 mL

1. Combine marinade ingredients and marinate turkey for 20 minutes.
2. Combine sauce ingredients and set aside.
3. In large non-stick skillet or wok, heat oil over medium-high heat. Add onions, garlic and ginger and stir-fry for 30 seconds.
4. Add turkey cubes and stir-fry until meat turns opaque and starts to brown, about 3 minutes. Add peppers and stir for 30 seconds. Add stock and continue to stir-fry for 1 minute.
5. Increase heat to high. Add sauce mixture and almonds and cook until sauce is thickened and almost absorbed. Serve immediately.

Serves 4

Each serving provides:

	Calories	316
g	Carbohydrates	10
g	Protein	36
g	Fat	14
g	Saturated Fat	3
mg	Cholesterol	86
g	Fibre	1
mg	Sodium	623
mg	Potassium	475

Excellent: vitamin E
Good: niacin; vitamin B-6; vitamin B-12; iron

Pan-roasted Duck

Those glistening barbecued ducks hanging in Chinese-noodle shop windows are tempting, but you consider them off-limits, right? Then this recipe is for you. Here, pan-roasting gives us that succulent taste and removing the skin afterwards gets rid of nearly all the fat.

Duck and Marinade:

1 tsp	finely grated ginger	5 mL
½ tsp	minced garlic	2 mL
½ tsp	five-spice powder	2 mL
1 tbsp	hoisin sauce	15 mL
¼ tsp	salt	1 mL
1 tbsp	dry sherry	15 mL
1 tbsp	honey	15 mL
1½ tsp	sesame oil	7 mL
1 tbsp	Chicken Stock (p. 3) or water	15 mL
4	boneless duck breasts, skin on	4

1. Heat small saucepan over low heat. Add all marinade ingredients and heat until honey is melted and well mixed .

2. Place duck breasts (with skin on) and marinade in large self-sealing or freezer bag. Squeeze to remove all air and seal. Rub marinade onto duck breast and under skin through freezer bag and refrigerate for 4 hours or overnight.

3. Preheat oven to 400°F/200°C.

4. Remove duck from marinade and prick skin with fork several times. Boil marinade for 5 minutes and reserve for basting.

5. In non-stick ovenproof skillet over medium-high heat, fry duck breast skin-side down until golden brown, about 2 minutes. Pour off rendered fat. Turn and brown meat side for about 2 minutes. Baste both sides and under skin with marinade. Pour off excess fat.

6. Place pan in heated oven and roast duck, skin-side up, for 15 minutes. Remove from oven and let rest for 5 minutes over warm oven vent.

7. Remove skin from meat. Slice duck breasts into bite-sized slices. Serve with Chinese Coleslaw (p. 122).

Serves 4

Each serving provides:		
	Calories	243
g	Carbohydrates	5
g	Protein	34
g	Fat	9
g	Saturated Fat	2
mg	Cholesterol	128
g	Fibre	tr
mg	Sodium	396
mg	Potassium	482

Excellent: thiamine; riboflavin; vitamin B-6; vitamin B-12; iron

Good: niacin; folacin

Braised Pork Tenderloin with Chayote

Chayote
Buddha's hand melon, mirliton

Chayote squash has shiny, light green skin and mild white flesh that secretes a white sap when cut. When braised or stir-fried it is sweet and delicious. Before use, peel off the thin skin, cut in half along the slash and pry out the large seed as you would with an avocado.

A fond memory came to me recently. I hadn't had this dish since I was a child. When I visited Hong Kong a few years ago I fell in love with it all over again. Seafood like prawns and squid can be added; chunks of squash or carrots can also go in for colour and variety. Use zucchini if you can't find chayote—just shorten the cooking time.

Pork and Marinade:

1 lb	pork tenderloin, trimmed of fat, cut in medallions ¹/₂-inch/1 cm thick	500 g
2 tsp	minced garlic	10 mL
1 tbsp	minced ginger	15 mL
¹/₂ tsp	five-spice powder	2 mL
¹/₄ tsp	salt	1 mL
2 tbsp	dry sherry	25 mL
1 tbsp	cornstarch	15 mL
1¹/₂ tsp	canola oil	7 mL
1 cup	Chicken Stock (p. 3) or Rich Pork Stock (p. 8)	250 mL
3	medium chayotes, peeled, or 4 zucchinis, cut in fingers	3
1¹/₂ tsp	fish sauce	7 mL
¹/₂ tsp	sugar	2 mL
¹/₄ tsp	white pepper	1 mL

1. Combine marinade ingredients with pork medallions and marinate for 30 minutes.
2. Heat non-stick skillet or wok over high heat and add oil. Add medallions and fry until golden, about 1 minute on each side. Remove and keep warm.
3. Pour stock into pan and stir. Add chayote and bring to boil. Season with fish sauce, sugar and pepper. Reduce heat to medium, cover and braise for 20 minutes or until chayote is tender. Add more stock if necessary.
4. Increase heat to high, add pork and mix well. Cook for 1 minute or until sauce is slightly thickened. Arrange pork medallions attractively with chayotes and serve.

Serves 4

Each serving provides:

	Calories	269
g	Carbohydrates	12
g	Protein	36
g	Fat	8
g	Saturated Fat	3
mg	Cholesterol	108
g	Fibre	5
mg	Sodium	251
mg	Potassium	772

Excellent: thiamine; riboflavin; niacin; vitamin B-6; vitamin B-12; zinc
Good: fibre; vitamin C; folacin; iron

Beef with Tomatoes and Green Beans

Tomatoes, like yams and chili peppers, likely arrived in China around the 1500s. Spanish and Portuguese travellers brought them from the New World via Indonesia and the Philippines. Now the use of these fan *(an unflattering word for foreign) vegetables is widespread. The Chinese generally do not peel tomatoes, but if you like to do so, see sidebar for instructions.*

Beef and Marinade:

½ lb	lean sirloin beef, thinly sliced	250 g
1 tbsp	soy sauce	15 mL
½ tsp	sugar	2 mL
1 tbsp	dry sherry	15 mL
¼ tsp	black pepper	1 mL
1½ tsp	cornstarch	7 mL
1 tbsp	canola oil	15 mL
1 lb	fresh roma tomatoes, cut in quarters	500 g
1	small onion, sliced	1
2 tsp	minced garlic	10 mL
1 tsp	minced ginger	5 mL
½ lb	green beans, trimmed and sliced diagonally in 2-inch/5 cm segments	250 g

1. Combine beef with marinade ingredients and marinate for 20 minutes.
2. Heat non-stick skillet or wok over medium-high heat and add oil. Sear beef, separating slices for even cooking, about 1 minute or until medium rare. Remove from pan and set aside.
3. Add tomatoes, onions, garlic and ginger and cook for 1 minute. Add green beans and stir to mix. Cover and cook for 3 minutes or until beans are tender. Add beef and stir to mix well for 1 minute. Transfer to deep dish and serve.

Serves 4

To Peel Tomatoes

Score the bottom of each tomato lightly in the shape of a small cross, just deep enough to break the skin. Put tomatoes in boiling water and blanch briefly, about 45 seconds. Remove with a slotted spoon and cool under cold running water. Skin will peel off easily from the cut edges.

Each serving provides:

	Calories	183
g	Carbohydrates	14
g	Protein	16
g	Fat	7
g	Saturated Fat	2
mg	Cholesterol	38
g	Fibre	4
mg	Sodium	301
mg	Potassium	600

Excellent: vitamin C; vitamin B-12; zinc
Good: vitamin A; folacin; iron; fibre; niacin; vitamin B-6

Spicy Beef with Baby Bok Choy

See photo, page 65

Great on its own or over those flat rice noodles called sha ho fun, *this is my favourite beef dish by far. And it looks good too, as you can see from the photo. Use* bok choy sum *("heart of bok choy"), baby bok choy, gai lan or even regular broccoli for a real taste treat.*

Satay Sauce
Sha Cha Chiang
(sand tea sauce)

Traders introduced this Southeast Asian import to China over a thousand years ago. It contains various proportions of dried fish and shrimp, garlic, chilies, coriander, star anise and peanuts. I use the one with a gold label and a Panda logo. It's a great, versatile sauce to keep in your pantry and can be used by itself for barbecued meats and shellfish.

Beef and Marinade:

¾ lb	lean beef (flank steak), thinly sliced	375 g
1 tbsp	soy sauce	15 mL
1 tbsp	cornstarch	15 mL
½ tsp	sugar	2 mL
2 tbsp	water	25 mL
1 tbsp	dry sherry	15 mL

Sauce:

¼ cup	Veal Demi-glace (p. 7) or Chicken Stock (p. 3)	125 mL
2 tsp	oyster sauce	10 mL
1 tbsp	satay sauce	15 mL
1 tbsp	water	15 mL
1 tsp	cornstarch	5 mL
½ cup	Chicken Stock or Vegetable Stock (p. 4)	125 mL
1 lb	baby bok choy, washed, trimmed, cut finger length	500 g
½ tsp	sugar, optional	2 mL
1 tbsp	minced garlic	15 mL
1 tsp	sesame oil	5 mL
1 tbsp	canola oil	15 mL
6	thick slices ginger	6
2	large shallots, thinly sliced	2
2	red chilies, optional	2

1. Marinate beef in marinade for at least 30 minutes or overnight.
2. Combine sauce ingredients and set aside.
3. Heat wok and stock on medium-high heat, add bok choy, sugar and garlic and stir-fry for 1 minute. Cover to cook for 2 minutes or until bok choy is just tender. Uncover and stir briefly until liquid is absorbed, about 1 minute. Add sesame oil and toss to mix. Remove vegetables and keep warm. Rinse and dry wok.
4. To cook beef, heat wok on high heat and add oil. When oil begins smoking, add ginger, shallots and chilies and fry briefly until fragrant. Add beef and stir to cook evenly for 1 to 2 minutes or until beef begins to turn pale. Add sauce mixture and stir-fry for about 1 minute until sauce has thickened. Pour evenly over vegetables or stir in with vegetables and serve immediately.

Serves 4

Each serving provides:		
	Calories	288
g	Carbohydrates	11
g	Protein	27
g	Fat	15
g	Saturated Fat	4
mg	Cholesterol	72
g	Fibre	1
mg	Sodium	756
mg	Potassium	738

Excellent: vitamin C; vitamin B-12; vitamin B-6; vitamin A; folacin; zinc; iron
Good: riboflavin; niacin

Lamb Ossobuco Chinese Style

The Chinese believe that eating gelatinous cuts of meat, or anything gelatinous for that matter, will keep you supple. I just love ossobuco for its taste and texture, hence this cross-cultural dish.

You can substitute beef or veal shank in this recipe and, if you like, other root vegetables or squashes can be added for variety. If you want it a little spicy, add a few slices of red chili peppers or one or two dried chilies. It makes a hearty meal served with Gingered Brown Rice (p. 29).

Braising Liquid:

1-inch	knob ginger, smashed	2.5 cm
2 tsp	five-spice powder	10 mL
2	pieces dried tangerine peel, rinsed	2
2 tbsp	mushroom soy sauce	25 mL
2 cups	Chicken Stock (p. 3)	500 mL
1 tbsp	canola oil	15 mL
8	small whole shallots, peeled	8
4	cloves garlic, peeled	4
1½ lb	boneless lamb shank, sliced in 6 pieces	750 g
⅓ cup	flour	75 mL
½ cup	dry sherry or white wine	125 mL
6-inch	segment white daikon or turnip	15 cm
1	small green daikon or turnip	1
1	large carrot	1
5	thick slices ginger	5
4	green onions, cut in quarters	4
1 tbsp	balsamic or Chinese black vinegar	15 mL

Daikon
Chinese white radish, icicle radish, lo bak

This large radish comes in white and green. The white variety is larger (a foot or longer) and is light and slightly sweet when added to stews and soups. The green variety is smaller and slightly starchy and has a sharper flavour—I prefer it in braised dishes. Turnips are an excellent substitute for both.

1. Peel daikons or turnips and carrots and cut into equal-sized large chunks.
2. Combine all ingredients for braising liquid in medium saucepan and bring to boil. Reduce heat to low and simmer.
3. Heat oil in heavy non-stick skillet. Add shallots and garlic and saute until golden.
4. Dredge lamb pieces in flour until well coated. Add lamb pieces to skillet and brown meat on all sides. Remove from skillet and add to braising liquid. Cover and simmer, stirring occasionally.
5. Add sherry and vegetables to skillet. Cook for 2 minutes or until liquid is absorbed. Set aside.
6. After meat has cooked for 30 minutes, add vegetable mixture and continue cooking over low heat for about 30 minutes or until lamb shanks and vegetables are tender when tested with a fork. Stir periodically to ensure even cooking. If liquid becomes too thick, add small amounts of water. When meat is done, remove tangerine peel and ginger.
7. To serve, heat Chinese clay pot or cast-iron pan until very hot. Throw in ginger and green onions, then add vinegar and hot stew to pot. Stir briefly to mix, and bring to vigorous boil. Serve while sizzling.

Serves 6

Each serving provides:		
	Calories	257
g	Carbohydrates	13
g	Protein	22
g	Fat	12
g	Saturated Fat	4
mg	Cholesterol	72
g	Fibre	1
mg	Sodium	497
mg	Potassium	446

Excellent: zinc; vitamin A; vitamin C; vitamin B-12
Good: iron; folacin

Venison Medallions with Pickled Ginger

The Chinese believe venison is pu—*fortifying and warming—to the body. Ginger and pepper are classic flavourings to mitigate the strong flavour of the meat and to enhance the "heating" effects. Venison was such a precious meat that it was used as an allegory for conquest—fighting for disputed territory was called "chasing after the deer."*

1 tbsp	soy sauce	15 mL
1/2 cup	Veal Demi-glace (p. 7) Chicken Stock (p. 3)	125 mL
2 tsp	cornstarch	10 mL
3/4 lb	venison loin, cut across grain in 1/2-inch/1.25 cm medallions	375 g
1/4 tsp	salt	1 mL
2 tsp	coarse black pepper, freshly ground	10 mL
1 tbsp	canola oil	15 mL
2 tbsp	dry sherry	25 mL
2	cloves garlic, thinly sliced	2
1	small onion, sliced	1
8	slices pickled ginger, cut in threads	8
1 tbsp	pickling liquid from ginger	15 mL
1	large green bell pepper, seeded and cut in large dice	1
1	small red bell pepper, seeded and cut in large dice	1

1. Mix soy sauce, stock and cornstarch and set aside.
2. Season venison medallions with salt and coat well with black pepper.
3. Heat non-stick skillet or wok over high heat. Add oil and heat. Add venison pieces to sear until medium rare, about 1 minute on each side. Remove and set aside to rest.
4. Add sherry, garlic, onions, ginger and ginger liquid and stir for 30 seconds.
5. Add peppers and stir to mix for 30 seconds. Add soy sauce mixture, stir to mix well, and cover to cook for 1 minute or until peppers are ten-der-crisp.
6. Add venison and juices to vegetables, stir and mix well. Cook for about 1 minute or until sauce is slightly thickened. Arrange venison attractively over peppers and serve immediately.

Serves 4

Three Bean Ragout with Curry-fried Tofu, page 109 >

Did you know that...

- Boat For Hope has raised $290,000 for children who have special needs and directed $50,000 to Down Syndrome Research Foundation.
- Boat For Hope has hosted 1,400 children for a day of fun on the water.
- Variety has supported over 2,000 organizations and hundreds of individual children and their families.
- Variety has provided grants for Greater Victoria Hospital Foundation, YWCA Crabtree Corner, Quesnel & District Child Development Association.
- Over 460 Sunshine Coaches have been placed throughout BC.
- More than 10,000 dedicated volunteers help Variety help kids at over 200 events that are held annually throughout the province.

Thank you for helping Variety - The Children's Charity help kids!
www.boatforhope.com

What's a day without hope?

in support of

VARIETY
The Children's Charity

Variety - The Children's Charity of BC,
raises funds for the purpose of
advancing the health, happiness,
and well-being of BC's children in need.

Please help Variety help kids with a $3 donation to Boat For Hope.

Spicy Tangerine Beef

Beef and Marinade:

3	large pieces dried tangerine peel	3
1 ½ lb	top sirloin or New York steak	750 g
½ cup	boiling water	125 mL
3	large cloves garlic, minced	3
2	green onions, cut in quarters	2
2-inch	knob fresh ginger, smashed	5 cm
2 tsp	oyster sauce	10 mL
2 tsp	soy sauce	10 mL
3 tbsp	dry sherry	45 mL
2 tbsp	orange juice concentrate	25 mL
2 tsp	Vietnamese chili sauce	10 mL
1 tsp	Worcestershire sauce	5 mL
1 tsp	sugar	5 mL
1 tbsp	cornstarch	15 mL
2 tbsp	water	25 mL
6	orange slices	6
3	sprigs fresh cilantro	3

1. Soak dried tangerine peel in hot water for about 10 minutes. Chop, return to liquid and mash mixture to extract flavour.
2. In shallow dish or self-sealing bag, combine all marinade ingredients, including tangerine peel mixture. Add steak and refrigerate at least 2 hours or overnight.
3. Preheat barbecue to high.
4. Remove steak from marinade and brush off solids. Strain marinade through fine strainer and set aside for basting. Grill steaks on oiled rack to degree of doneness you want, basting once or twice on each side. Or pan-fry or broil steaks in a very hot pan with 1 tbsp/15 mL canola oil. Timing is the same: about 2 minutes for each side (this increases calories to 290 and fat to 11 g per serving). Allow steaks to rest for 2 to 3 minutes when done.
5. Meanwhile, add 2 tbsp/25 mL water to remaining marinade and boil for 1 minute or until sauce is reduced and slightly thickened.
6. Cut cooked steaks into thin slices. To serve, pour sauce over steak slices and garnish with orange slices and cilantro. Serve immediately.

Serves 6

< *Lychee Granita*, page 130

Tangerine Peel

Good-quality tangerine peel from China will give much better flavour to your dishes. Buy it from Chinese apothecary shops and you'll have an excuse to poke around and find out about all those strange things they have on display and in little drawers. If you are interested in dietary cures and Chinese medicine, many of these shops have their own resident herbalist/doctor in residence.

Each serving provides:

	Calories	270
g	Carbohydrates	9
g	Protein	35
g	Fat	9
g	Saturated Fat	4
mg	Cholesterol	101
g	Fibre	1
mg	Sodium	354
mg	Potassium	601

Excellent: iron; zinc; vitamin B-6; vitamin B-12
Good: vitamin C; riboflavin; niacin

Steamed Pork in Egg Custard

Instead of custard, the Chinese call this country dish a "meat cake" and steam it over the cooking rice to conserve energy. I sometimes think of it as a cross between a meatloaf and a pâté with eggs. It's wonderful on rice. To further reduce fat, replace whole eggs with 4 egg whites.

Minced Pork

Place pork loin in freezer for about 1 to 2 hours to freeze slightly. Then slice into thin slices and chop with a heavy knife or Chinese cleaver. This will make a coarser mince than you would get from a food processor, but it's the texture Chinese cooks prefer.

Pork Mixture:

½ lb	lean minced pork	250 g
1 tsp	soy sauce	5 mL
½ tsp	sesame oil	2 mL
½ tsp	pepper	2 mL
1 tsp	finely chopped cilantro	5 mL
1 tbsp	finely chopped green onion	15 mL
1 tbsp	minced ginger	15 mL
1½ tsp	cornstarch	7 mL

Egg Mixture:

2	large eggs, beaten	2
½ cup	Chicken Stock (p. 3) or Rich Pork Stock (p. 8)	125 mL
¼ tsp	salt	1 mL
¼ tsp	canola oil	1 mL
1 tbsp	finely chopped green onion	15 mL
1	sprig cilantro, chopped or left whole, for garnish	1

1. In deep ovenproof dish that fits in steamer, combine pork mixture ingredients. Flatten meat mixture to cover bottom of dish.
2. In bowl, stir together egg mixture ingredients.
3. Pour egg mixture over meat and skim off bubbles. Place in steamer and steam over medium-high heat for 10 minutes. Turn off heat and let custard settle, covered, for 5 minutes. Garnish with cilantro and serve.

Serves 4

Each serving provides:

	Calories	128
g	Carbohydrates	2
g	Protein	16
g	Fat	6
g	Saturated Fat	2
mg	Cholesterol	142
mg	Fibre	tr
mg	Sodium	288
mg	Potassium	248

Excellent: thiamine; vitamin B-12
Good: riboflavin; vitamin B-6; zinc

Beef in Sweet and Sour Sauce

This dish is even quicker and easier if you prepare the meat the night before. The light sweet and sour sauce can be used for chicken and tastes great with fish. Veal Demi-glace is optional but will add depth of flavour to the beef; however, chicken stock is quite acceptable. Use light soy sauce for chicken and fish.

Beef and Marinade:

¾ lb	sirloin tip, trimmed, cut in thin slices	375 g
1½ tsp	soy sauce	7 mL
1½ tsp	mushroom soy sauce	7 mL
½ tsp	pepper	2 mL
1 tsp	cornstarch	5 mL
1 tbsp	dry sherry	15 mL

Sauce:

1 tbsp	Worcestershire sauce	15 mL
2 tbsp	tomato ketchup	25 mL
1½ tsp	sugar	7 mL
2 tbsp	Veal Demi-glace (p. 7) or Chicken Stock (p. 3)	25 mL
½ tsp	sesame oil	2 mL
½ tsp	cornstarch	2 mL
1 tbsp	canola oil	15 mL
1	large onion, sliced	1
2	small tomatoes, sliced	2

1. Marinate steak in marinade for at least 2 hours or overnight.
2. Combine sauce ingredients and set aside.
3. Heat oil in non-stick skillet over high heat. Add onions and saute for 2 minutes or until golden. Remove and set aside.
4. Add steak slices and saute for 30 seconds on each side. Add tomato slices and stir for about 1 minute. Add sauce ingredients and bring to boil. Cook until sauce thickens slightly. Serve.

Serves 4

Soy Sauce

Light and dark refer to the colour of the soy sauce and not the salt content. They are made by fermenting roasted soy beans and wheat and then adding brine. Dark soy sauce has been aged longer and has molasses added, giving it its colour and slightly sweet taste. The general rule is to use the light sauce for light meats and the dark for dark meats. Flavoured soy sauces like mushroom soy have deep, subtle flavours.

Each serving provides:

	Calories	260
g	Carbohydrates	12
g	Protein	27
g	Fat	11
g	Saturated Fat	3
mg	Cholesterol	76
g	Fibre	1
mg	Sodium	453
mg	Potassium	624

Excellent: vitamin B-12; iron; zinc

Good: riboflavin; niacin; vitamin B-6

Pork-stuffed Mo Qua

Mo Qua
Hairy or fuzzy melon, tseet gwa

It looks like a fuzzy zucchini with light green skin but is a closer relative of the winter melon. The pale green flesh is delicious and versatile. Just peel off the tough skin, scoop out the seeds if you wish, and it's ready to be put in anything from stir-fries to stews to soups. Cucumbers can be substituted in a pinch.

1	2 oz/60 g package cellophane noodles	1
2	mo qua or English cucumbers	2

Pork and Marinade:

1/2 lb	Minced Pork (p. 94)	250 g
1/4 tsp	salt	1 mL
1 tbsp	minced ginger	15 mL
2 tbsp	chopped cilantro	25 mL
1	egg white, slightly beaten	1
1 1/2 tsp	cornstarch	7 mL
1/2 tsp	sesame oil	2 mL

Sauce:

1 tbsp	oyster sauce	15 mL
1 cup	Rich Pork Stock (p. 8) or Chicken Stock (p. 3)	250 mL
1 tsp	hot red pepper flakes	5 mL
4	large shiitake mushroom caps, thinly sliced	4

1. Cover cellophane noodles with hot water and soak for 10 minutes or until noodles are soft. Drain well and chop coarsely.
2. Peel and cut mo qua crosswise into 1-inch/2.5 cm slices. Scoop out some seeds and pulp from centre of each slice to form bowl.
3. Combine pork and marinade ingredients with half of cellophane noodles. Spoon meat mixture into mo qua "bowl" and press down gently to cover slice with small, smooth mound of mixture. Dip each stuffed piece of mo qua meat-side down into remaining cellophane noodles until well coated.
4. Heat skillet over medium-high heat and add sauce ingredients. Add stuffed mo qua slices squash-side down. Cover and braise for total of 15 minutes. After first 5 minutes of cooking, uncover and spoon sauce over meat. Cover and continue cooking. Repeat basting after another 5 minutes and add mushroom slices. Cook for 5 more minutes.
5. Remove mo qua slices and arrange on platter. Pour sauce over and serve. If sauce is too thin, thicken after removing the mo qua, then pour over stuffed squash.

Serves 4

Each serving provides:

	Calories	183
g	Carbohydrates	22
g	Protein	16
g	Fat	4
g	Saturated Fat	1
mg	Cholesterol	36
g	Fibre	3
mg	Sodium	357
mg	Potassium	508

Excellent: thiamine

Good: fibre; niacin; B-6; zinc

Barbecued Pork

Capture the flavour of the Chinese butcher's barbecued pork, but without the high fat and salt content. Letting the meat sit in the liquid after simmering helps very lean cuts of meat to retain their moisture.

6 cups	water	1.5 L
2 lb	boneless pork loin, cut lengthwise in 2-inch/5 cm strips	1 kg

Marinade:

2 tbsp	soy sauce	25 mL
1 1/2 tsp	Chinese red bean curd	7 mL
5	slices ginger	5
2	green onions, coarsely chopped and smashed	2
4	cloves garlic, peeled, smashed	4
2 tbsp	sherry	25 mL
3 tbsp	honey, divided	45 mL

1. In saucepan, put water and pork pieces. Heat on medium until contents reach low boil.
2. Reduce heat to low and simmer covered for 10 minutes. Turn off heat and let meat sit in liquid for another 10 minutes.
3. In large glass or plastic bowl or self-sealing bag, combine all marinade ingredients but 1 tbsp/15 mL honey. Remove pork pieces from water, pat dry with paper towels and add to marinade. Marinate in refrigerator for at least 4 hours or overnight.
4. Remove pork from marinade. Transfer marinade to saucepan and reduce on high heat to 1/2 volume. Add remaining 1 tbsp/15 mL honey. Roll pork pieces in reduced marinade to coat evenly.
5. Heat oven broiler to high. Set up rack in roasting pan. Place pork pieces on rack and broil for 3 minutes on each side or until golden. Baste meat with remaining marinade once or twice during cooking. Or cook marinated meat on the barbecue over high heat, turning often to prevent burning.
6. Remove pork from oven and allow to rest for 5 minutes. Slice and serve hot or allow to cool and use in other recipes.

Serves 6

Red Bean Curd
Chinese red bean curd, nam yu

This is one of a few varieties of preserved bean curd used for cooking or just eating in China. Some people even put the white variety on toast like peanut butter! Red bean curd's flavour is somewhere between miso and a ripe cheese. Red miso can be used as a substitute but the flavour pales in comparison. It's worth seeking out the real thing because an opened jar keeps indefinitely in the refrigerator.

Each serving provides:

	Calories	279
g	Carbohydrates	11
g	Protein	35
g	Fat	10
g	Saturated Fat	4
mg	Cholesterol	98
g	Fibre	tr
mg	Sodium	437
mg	Potassium	471

Excellent: thiamine; niacin; vitamin B-6; vitamin B-12; zinc
Good: riboflavin

Lamb and Leek Rolls

The original Chinese pancakes are painstaking to make, so flour tortillas have become the stand-in at my house.

To clean the leeks, simply slice them into thin strips, put the whole lot in a strainer and rinse really well with cold water to get rid of the dirt that may be hiding between the leaves—much easier than trying to clean them when they're whole.

¾ lb	lamb loin, thinly sliced	375 g
¼ tsp	black pepper	1 mL

Sauce:

1½ tsp	hot bean paste	7 mL
1 tbsp	hoisin sauce	15 mL
3½ tbsp	Chicken Stock (p. 3) or Veal Demi-glace (p. 7)	65 mL
2 tsp	cornstarch	10 mL
1 tbsp	canola oil	15 mL
1	clove garlic, thinly sliced	1
½ cup	Chicken Stock	125 mL
4 cups	thinly sliced leeks	1 L
12	flour tortillas	12

1. Season lamb slices with pepper and set aside.
2. Combine sauce ingredients and set aside.
3. Heat oil in large non-stick skillet over medium-high heat. Add lamb slices and saute until medium rare, about 45 seconds on each side. Remove lamb from pan.
4. Add garlic and stir to cook for 30 seconds. Add sauce ingredients and bring to boil. Continue to cook until sauce just begins to thicken. Remove sauce from pan and set aside.
5. Add stock to pan and bring to boil. Add leeks and cook until tender and liquid is absorbed, about 3 minutes.
6. Stir in lamb and sauce and cook until liquid is almost absorbed. Transfer to platter.
7. To serve, warm tortillas in dry, hot frying pan until lightly toasted but still pliable. Have diners help themselves by spooning small portion of lamb mixture onto tortillas and rolling up with one end folded in to avoid dripping.

Serves 4

Hoisin Sauce

Hoisin is one of many flavoured prepared soybean sauces commonly used in Chinese cooking. It generally contains garlic, five-spice powder, sugar, chilies and sometimes sweet potatoes. It's the classic condiment for Peking duck, but also adds sweet, rich flavour to chicken, meat and seafood dishes.

Each serving provides:

	Calories	315
g	Carbohydrates	27
g	Protein	24
g	Fat	13
g	Saturated Fat	3
mg	Cholesterol	64
g	Fibre	4
mg	Sodium	658
mg	Potassium	360

Excellent: vitamin B-12; iron

Good: fibre; niacin; folacin

Miso Pork with Water Chestnuts and Snow Peas

See photo, page 66

Red miso and Japanese seven-spice add a nice touch to this colourful stir-fry. The water chestnuts add sweetness and crunch to this summery dish. Be careful not to overcook the snow peas.

Pork and Marinade:

¾ lb	pork loin, thinly sliced	375 g
1 tbsp	Rich Pork Stock (p. 8) or Chicken Stock (p. 3)	15 mL
¼ tsp	salt	1 mL
½ tsp	Japanese seven-spice	2 mL
1 tbsp	cornstarch	15 mL

Sauce:

1 tbsp	red miso paste	15 mL
⅔ cup	Rich Pork Stock or Chicken Stock	150 mL
1½ tsp	soy sauce	7 mL
2 tsp	cornstarch	10 mL
1 tbsp	canola oil	15 mL
3	slices ginger	3
1	carrot, cut in thin diagonal slices	1
¼ cup	Rich Pork Stock or Chicken Stock	50 mL
½ lb	snow peas, cleaned and trimmed	250 g
8-10	water chestnuts, fresh or canned, peeled and thinly sliced	8-10

1. Combine pork with marinade ingredients and set aside.
2. Combine sauce ingredients and set aside.
3. Heat oil in large non-stick skillet over medium-high heat. Add ginger and saute for 30 seconds. Add pork and saute for 2 minutes or until pork is lightly browned. Reduce heat to medium, add sauce ingredients and cook for 1 minute or until sauce just begins to thicken. Remove pork and sauce from pan and set aside.
4. To same pan, add carrots and stock and cook for 1 minute. Add snow peas and water chestnuts and stir-fry for 2 minutes or until vegetables are tender-crisp.
5. Add pork mixture, stir to mix well and cook until warmed through. Serve immediately.

Serves 4

Water Chestnuts

Let me go on the record. Fresh water chestnuts are far better than the pale imitations in cans. Fresh ones are a lot more trouble to prepare when all you want is to get dinner over with, but for special occasions, they're worth it—so crunchy, sweet and juicy I used to eat them like a fruit. Choose water chestnuts that are shiny and hard, peel them with a sharp knife and put them in water with a light squeeze of lemon to prevent them from going brown.

Each serving provides:

	Calories	210
g	Carbohydrates	13
g	Protein	21
g	Fat	8
g	Saturated Fat	2
mg	Cholesterol	54
g	Fibre	2
mg	Sodium	391
mg	Potassium	508

Excellent: vitamin A; vitamin C; thiamine; vitamin B-6; vitamin B-12

Good: vitamin E; riboflavin; niacin; folacin; iron; zinc

Each serving provides:

	Calories	264
g	Carbohydrates	21
g	Protein	26
g	Fat	9
g	Saturated Fat	3
mg	Cholesterol	38
g	Fibre	2
mg	Sodium	471
mg	Potassium	692

Excellent: vitamin C; riboflavin; vitamin B-6; vitamin B-12; calcium; iron
Good: thiamine

Beef and Prawns with Chinese Celery and Lychees

The crunchy Chinese celery and sweet lychees provide a refreshing contrast to the chili sauce and the beef. Asparagus is also very good in this dish.

Beef and Marinade:

½ lb	beef flank steak, thinly sliced	250 g
1 tbsp	oyster sauce	15 mL
2 tsp	cornstarch	10 mL
1 tbsp	sherry	15 mL
1 ½ tsp	canola oil	7 mL
1 ½ tsp	hot bean paste	7 mL
2 tsp	minced ginger	10 mL
½	medium onion, sliced	½
½ lb	tiger prawns, shelled and deveined, 12 to 16	250 g
4 cups	Chinese celery or celery with leaves, cut in 2-inch/5 cm lengths	1 L
¼ cup	Chicken Stock (p. 3)	50 mL
1 cup	canned lychees, halved, with 2 tbsp/25 mL juice	250 mL

1. Combine beef with marinade ingredients and marinate for 20 minutes.
2. Heat oil in non-stick skillet or wok over high heat. Add hot bean paste, ginger and onions and saute for 30 seconds.
3. Add beef, stirring to separate pieces, and saute for 2 minutes. Turn only once or twice to allow to brown. Add prawns and stir-fry for 1 minute until prawns are just turning pink. Remove mixture.
4. Add Chinese celery and stock to skillet and stir for 30 seconds. Cover and cook for 1 minute.
5. Return beef and prawn mixture to skillet, add lychee liquid and stir to mix until sauce is thickened, about 1 minute.
6. Remove from heat. Add lychees, carefully stir together and serve.

Serves 4

Baked Tofu Rolls
with Pea Sprouts and Shrimp

Tofu Skin Wraps
Tofu skin, bean curd
skin, fu jook

These are the sheets
that form on top of
hot soy milk when it
is allowed to stand.
They come fresh-
frozen in large
translucent rounds
or rectangles that
roughly resemble
waxed paper. These
are the easiest to
work with for rolls
and dim sum items.
Others come in rolled
or pleated sticks and
are mostly used in
soups or braised and
stir-fried dishes.

The contrast of crispy tofu skin and soft filling makes this a delicious
way to enjoy tofu. Other combinations, like ground pork and spinach
or strips of chicken and Chinese chives, are also good fillings.

1 lb	medium tofu	500 g

Prawns and Marinade:

1/2 lb	prawns, shelled and deveined, coarsely chopped	250 g
2 tbsp	dry sherry	25 mL
1/2 tsp	salt	2 mL
1 tbsp	soy sauce	15 mL
1/4 tsp	white pepper	1 mL
1 tbsp	cornstarch	15 mL
1 tsp	sesame oil	5 mL
1 tbsp	minced garlic	15 mL
3 tbsp	minced ginger	45 mL
1 cup	fresh or canned bamboo shoots, cut in thin strips	250 mL
1/4 lb	pea sprouts or chopped pea tops	125 g
2	sheets 20-inch/50 cm frozen round tofu skin	2
1	egg white, beaten	1
1 tbsp	canola oil	15 mL

1. Preheat oven to 325°F/180°C. Set wire rack on baking sheet and heat.
2. Pat tofu dry, cut into ½-inch/1 cm cubes and set aside.
3. Combine prawns with marinade ingredients and marinate for 10 minutes.
4. In non-stick skillet or wok, heat sesame oil over medium heat. Add garlic, ginger and prawns and saute for 1 minute or until prawns just start to turn opaque. Add bamboo shoots and stir-fry for 30 seconds. Add fresh tofu and gently toss until tofu is warmed through, about 1 minute. Remove and cool.
5. Gently fold pea sprouts into cooled tofu-shrimp mixture in mixing bowl.
6. To prepare rolls, cut each tofu skin into 6 wedges. Place about 2 tbsp/25 mL of filling on wide end of wedge, about 1 inch/2.5 cm from the base. Fold base edge over mixture, then fold about an inch of tofu skin on either side towards centre. Roll towards point to form a roll. Dampen point of tofu skin with beaten egg white to seal. Set on platter. Repeat procedure to make 12 rolls.
7. Heat 1½ tsp/7 mL canola oil in non-stick skillet over medium-high heat. Add 6 tofu rolls and pan-fry until crisp and golden, about 1 minute on each side. Set aside and repeat with other rolls.
8. Transfer completed rolls to rack in oven and bake for 5 minutes. Transfer to serving plate, cut with clean kitchen shears into bite-sized pieces if desired, and serve immediately.

Serves 6

Rolling Instructions

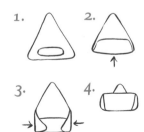

Each serving provides:

	Calories	256
g	Carbohydrates	13
g	Protein	26
g	Fat	13
g	Saturated Fat	2
mg	Cholesterol	74
g	Fibre	2
mg	Sodium	448
mg	Potassium	406

Excellent: iron; vitamin D; vitamin E; folacin; vitamin B-12; zinc

Good: thiamine; calcium

Pressed Tofu

Pressed tofu is simply
tofu that has been
pressed with weights
to squeeze out the
excess moisture. It
is firm and meatlike
and doesn't break
apart in stir-fries.
Some pressed tofu
comes seasoned or
fried. Avoid these if
you are concerned
about the extra salt
and higher fat con-
tent.

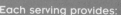

Each serving provides:

	Calories	280
g	Carbohydrates	31
g	Protein	21
g	Fat	10
g	Saturated Fat	1
mg	Cholesterol	tr
g	Fibre	6
mg	Sodium	298
mg	Potassium	511

Excellent: fibre; vitamin D;
folacin; iron; vitamin C
Good: vitamin E; thiamine;
vitamin B-6

Mushroom Tofu Stir-fry

*Take advantage of the different varieties of cultivated mushrooms
available year-round. If you can get foraged mushrooms such as
morels, chanterelles and others, use them in this recipe. You can bake it
in a phyllo parcel as a wonderful side dish for the most elegant western
dinner.*

4	medium dried Chinese mushrooms	4
½ cup	hot water	125 mL
2 tsp	cornstarch	10 mL
½ lb	pressed tofu, sliced ¼ inch/5 mm thick	250 g
1 tbsp	soy sauce	15 mL
1 tbsp	canola oil	15 mL
4	cloves garlic, chopped	4
2-inch	piece ginger, peeled, cut in thin strips	5 cm
½	red bell pepper, diced	½
½	bunch Chinese flowering chives, cut in matchsticks	½
¼ lb	oyster mushrooms, trimmed, torn in bite-sized strips	125 g
½ lb	snow peas, washed and trimmed	250 g
½ tsp	white pepper	2 mL
1 tsp	five-spice powder	5 mL
1	3.5-oz/100 g pkg enoki mushrooms	1
½ cup	bean sprouts	125 mL

1. Soak dried Chinese mushrooms in hot water for about 20 minutes
until plump and soft. Reserve and strain liquid; remove mushrooms,
slice thinly and set aside.
2. Whisk together cornstarch and cooled mushroom liquid until smooth.
3. Marinate tofu slices in soy sauce for 15 minutes. Remove tofu and
add soy sauce to thickened mushroom liquid.
4. Saute tofu slices in oil over medium-high heat for 1 minute on each
side or until golden brown. Remove tofu and set aside.
5. To pan, add mushroom strips, garlic, ginger, red bell pepper and
chives and stir for 1 minute until fragrant. Add oyster mushrooms and
snow peas and stir-fry for 1 minute.
6. Add mushroom liquid mixture and stir while sauce thickens. Season
with white pepper and five-spice powder and stir.
7. Return tofu to pan and add enoki mushrooms and bean sprouts. Stir
for 30 seconds and serve.

Serves 4

Tofu with Ground Pork

This one is hot! If you don't enjoy spicy food, you might want to use only half of the hot red pepper flakes called for, but the full teaspoon gives this dish its genuine Szechuan kick. It tastes terrific with hot steamed rice.

1 lb	soft tofu	500 g

Sauce:

½ cup	Rich Pork Stock (p. 8) or Chicken Stock (p. 3)	125 mL
2 tsp	soy sauce	10 mL
½ tsp	sesame oil	2 mL
1 tbsp	cornstarch	15 mL
1 tbsp	canola oil	15 mL
1 tbsp	minced garlic	15 mL
2 tbsp	chopped green onions	25 mL
1 tbsp	minced ginger	15 mL
1 tsp	hot red pepper flakes	5 mL
½ lb	lean pork, finely minced	250 g
½ tsp	pepper	2 mL
1 tbsp	dry sherry	15 mL

1. Dice tofu into ¼-inch/5 mm cubes, place in colander and drain well.
2. Whisk together sauce ingredients and set aside.
3. Heat oil in non-stick skillet or wok over high heat. Add garlic, green onions, ginger and hot pepper flakes and stir-fry for 30 seconds. Add pork, stir-fry for 1 minute and season with pepper and splash of sherry. Add sauce mixture and stir until sauce thickens.
4. Add tofu and stir gently to mix. Reduce heat to low, simmer for 3 minutes and serve.

Serves 4

Each serving provides:

	Calories	220
g	Carbohydrates	6
g	Protein	23
g	Fat	12
g	Saturated Fat	2
mg	Cholesterol	40
g	Fibre	2
mg	Sodium	209
mg	Potassium	370

Excellent: iron; vitamin E; thiamine

Good: vitamin B-6; vitamin B-12; zinc

Potsticker Tofu with Shrimp

A sizzling pan of deep-fried potstickers inspired this easy alternative. The result is a dish with the velvety texture of steamed tofu supported by a contrasting crispy bottom layer. This method also works well with the Fish Ball recipe on page 25 or the dumpling mixture on page 35.

1 lb	medium tofu, cut in ½-inch/1cm thick, 2-inch/5 cm squares	500 g
½ lb	raw shrimp, peeled and cleaned	250 g
2	egg whites	2
1 tbsp	fish sauce	15 mL
½ tsp	white pepper	2 mL
1½ tsp	cornstarch	7 mL
1 tbsp	finely chopped cilantro	15 mL
1 tbsp	finely chopped green onions	15 mL
1 tsp	minced ginger	5 mL
½ cup	Chicken Stock (p. 3)	125 mL
1	red chili, seeded and finely chopped	1
½ tsp	sesame oil	2 mL
½ tsp	pepper	2 mL
1 tbsp	canola oil	15 mL

1. Gently press tofu slices between paper towels to absorb surface moisture. Leave to dry while preparing shrimp paste.
2. In food processor, pulse shrimp, egg whites, fish sauce, white pepper and cornstarch into thick paste. To ensure shrimp is well blended, add a bit of chicken stock if necessary. Add cilantro, green onions and ginger and pulse briefly to mix. Set aside.
3. To remainder of chicken stock, add chopped chili and sesame oil.
4. Grind black pepper evenly onto large plate. Gently transfer tofu slices to plate and leave to season for 5 minutes.
5. Spread spoonful of shrimp paste onto each piece of tofu, pressing gently to secure.
6. Heat large heavy non-stick skillet over high heat. Add canola oil and heat until just beginning to smoke. Add prepared tofu pieces and fry for about 1 minute. Check to see if bottoms are beginning to brown.
7. Pour chicken stock mixture evenly over tofu pieces and cover to cook for about 3 minutes until liquid is mostly evaporated.
8. Uncover and continue cooking until liquid has evaporated and tofu pieces slide easily in pan. Transfer carefully to a plate and serve. Garnish with sprigs of cilantro if desired.

Serves 4

Each serving provides:

	Calories	197
g	Carbohydrates	4
g	Protein	24
g	Fat	10
g	Saturated Fat	1
mg	Cholesterol	113
g	Fibre	2
mg	Sodium	503
mg	Potassium	309

Excellent: vitamin E; vitamin D; iron; vitamin B-12
Good: zinc

Tofu with Lily Buds and Lotus Roots

The dried flower buds of the day lily (often called golden needles) are a major flavour element in Buddhist cooking, which uses no onions or garlic. I confess, I cheat by adding strong flavourings such as garlic and satay sauce to heighten the flavours here. Try this dish without these to return to its subtle roots.

¼ cup	dried lily buds	50 mL
¼ cup	dried cloud ear or Chinese mushrooms	50 mL
6-inch	piece fresh lotus root	15 cm
¾ lb	pressed tofu	375 g

Sauce:

1½ tsp	soy sauce	7 mL
½ tsp	satay sauce	2 mL
½ tsp	sesame oil	2 mL
1 tbsp	Chinese-style Vegetable Stock (p. 5)	15 mL
2 tsp	cornstarch	10 mL
1½ tsp	canola oil	7 mL
1 tsp	minced garlic	5 mL
1 tbsp	minced ginger	15 mL
½ cup	Chinese-style Vegetable Stock	125 mL
1	green onion, chopped	1

1. Soak lily buds and mushrooms separately in warm water for 20 minutes. Drain. Trim mushrooms and cut in bite-sized pieces.
2. Cut lotus root and tofu into ¼-inch/5 mm slices. Keep separate.
3. Combine sauce ingredients and set aside.
4. Heat oil in skillet over medium-high heat. Add garlic, ginger and lotus roots and stir-fry for 1 minute. Add stock and bring to boil. Cover to braise for 10 minutes.
5. Add lily buds, cloud ears and tofu and stir for 1 minute. Add green onions and sauce mixture. Stir to combine well, cook for 1 minute until sauce is slightly thickened and serve.

Serves 4

Lotus Root

The lotus flower, a symbol of purity, is cultivated all over Asia for its beauty and religious significance. The seeds, leaves and roots are used in cooking. Lotus root has a crunchy, starchy texture and an earthy flavour which resembles artichoke. Apart from adorning stir-fries with its pretty perforated slices, the Chinese also put it in stews and soups and preserve it as a candy for New Year.

Each serving provides:		
	Calories	273
g	Carbohydrates	35
g	Protein	18
g	Fat	12
g	Saturated Fat	1
mg	Cholesterol	0
g	Fibre	7
mg	Sodium	436
mg	Potassium	994

Excellent: calcium; iron; zinc; fibre; vitamin D; vitamin C; riboflavin; folacin

Good: thiamin; niacin; vitamin B-6

Braised Tofu with Barbecued Pork

This has become a weeknight staple for my family. If you don't have any homemade Barbecued Pork (p. 97), store-bought barbecued pork will do, but it will be a little fattier and saltier than our version. Compensate by choosing plain vegetables and rice to complete your meal.

8	dried Chinese mushrooms, soaked and thinly sliced	8
1 tbsp	cornstarch	15 mL
2 tbsp	Chicken Stock (p. 3) or water	25 mL
1 tbsp	canola oil	15 mL
5	slices ginger	5
3	green onions, cut in eighths	3
2 tsp	minced garlic	10 mL
¾ lb	Barbecued Pork (p. 97)	375 g
1 tbsp	oyster sauce	15 mL
1 tbsp	soy sauce	15 mL
¾ cup	Rich Pork Stock (p. 8) or Chicken Stock	175 mL
½ tsp	pepper, or to taste	2 mL
1 lb	soft tofu, in 1-by-½-inch/2.5-by-1 cm slices	500 g

1. As mushrooms soak, combine cornstarch and the 2 tbsp chicken stock and set aside.
2. Heat oil in wok over medium-high heat. Add ginger, green onions, garlic and mushrooms and saute until fragrant, about 1 minute. Add pork slices and stir-fry for about 1 minute. Add oyster sauce, soy sauce and stock. Reduce heat to medium. Mix well, cover and braise for 2 minutes. Season to taste with pepper. Add cornstarch mixture to thicken sauce.
3. Gently fold tofu into mixture. Cover to braise and allow tofu to absorb flavours for another 2 minutes, stirring occasionally. Transfer to deep platter and serve, or divide and serve over individual portions of steamed rice.

Serves 4

Three Bean Ragout
with Curry-fried Tofu

See photo, page 91

Tofu:

½ lb	medium tofu, in ½-by-1-inch/1-by-2.5 cm slices	250 g
2 tsp	curry powder	10 mL
⅛ tsp	salt	0.5 mL
1½ tsp	canola oil	7 mL

Bean Ragout:

¼ cup	finely chopped onions	50 mL
1 cup	soaked pinto beans (see method)	250 mL
½ lb	wax or green beans, trimmed, cut in thirds	250 g
1½ cups	frozen broad beans	375 mL
½ cup	Vegetable Stock (p. 4)	125 mL

Sauce:

1 tbsp	oyster sauce	15 mL
1 tsp	cornstarch	5 mL
2 tbsp	Vegetable Stock	25 mL
pinch	black pepper	pinch
1	tomato rose for garnish, optional	
1 tsp	chopped cilantro for garnish, optional	5 mL

1. Soak ½ cup/125 mL dried pinto beans in 2 cups/500 mL water overnight. In medium saucepan, bring beans and soaking liquid to boil and cook for 15 minutes or until beans are just tender. Drain and set aside.
2. Dry tofu pieces between paper towels. Mix curry powder and salt.
3. Heat oil in non-stick skillet over high heat. Dredge tofu pieces carefully in curry mixture until well coated. Fry for 1 minute on each side until golden brown. Remove from pan and keep warm.
4. Add all ragout ingredients to same pan, stir to mix, cover and cook over medium-high heat for 5 minutes or until green beans are tender. Add sauce mixture and stir until thickened, about 1 minute. Season with pepper.
5. Transfer bean ragout to serving platter or large pasta dish. Make dimple in centre of beans and fan tofu slices in centre. Garnish with tomato rose and cilantro and serve.

Serves 4

Tofu

Bean Smarts

Dried beans are an excellent source of soluble fibre. If you use canned beans for convenience, rinse them to eliminate salt.

Each serving provides:

	Calories	248
g	Carbohydrates	37
g	Protein	16
g	Fat	6
g	Saturated Fat	1
mg	Cholesterol	0
g	Fibre	12
mg	Sodium	248
mg	Potassium	726

Excellent: fibre; vitamin E; folacin; iron

Good: thiamine; riboflavin; vitamin B-6; calcium

Steamed Vegetarian Tofu Rolls

These flavour-packed rolls are delicious hot or cold—in fact, I like them better cold as an appetizer or side dish.

½ cup	dried Chinese mushrooms	125 mL
½ cup	hot water	125 mL

Filling:

1½ tsp	canola oil	7 mL
1 tsp	minced garlic	5 mL
2 tsp	minced ginger	10 mL
1 cup	bamboo shoots, fresh or canned, cut in matchsticks	250 mL
1 cup	yellow or green chives, cut in matchsticks	250 mL
1 cup	carrots, peeled, cut in 2-inch/5 cm matchsticks	250 mL
1	2-oz/60 g package cellophane noodles, soaked	1
1 tbsp	soy sauce	15 mL
2 tbsp	mirin or medium sherry	25 mL
¼ cup	mushroom liquid	50 mL
3 cups	shredded spinach leaves	750 mL
6	sheets frozen rectangular tofu skin wraps	6
1 tsp	sesame oil, divided	5 mL
1 tsp	hot bean paste	5 mL

1. Soak mushrooms in ½ cup/125 mL hot water for 20 minutes. Reserve and strain liquid. Remove mushrooms and slice thinly.
2. Heat wok over medium-high heat and add oil. Add garlic, ginger, mushrooms, bamboo shoots, chives and carrots and stir-fry for 2 minutes.
3. Push vegetables to one side, add cellophane noodles, soy sauce, mirin and mushroom liquid and stir-fry for 1 minute. Add spinach and stir to mix until liquid is absorbed, about 1 minute. Remove mixture and allow to cool slightly.
4. Set steamer over high heat. Brush plate with ½ tsp/2 mL sesame oil. Mix remaining sesame oil with hot bean paste and set aside.
5. Place sheet of tofu wrap on flat, dry surface. Spoon about ¼ cup/50 mL filling mixture onto bottom half of sheet. Fold bottom and side edges of sheet over filling and continue to form tight roll. Place on oiled plate seam-side down. Repeat to make 6 8-inch/20 cm rolls.
6. Place plate with rolls in steamer and steam for 5 minutes. When rolls are done, brush both sides with bean paste mixture while hot and serve hot or cold. Cut crosswise into 5 or 6 sections before serving.

Serves 6

Gai Lan with Oyster Sauce

Discover this wonder vegetable with its rich, nutty flavour and a slight hint of bitterness which makes it stand up admirably on its own. When lightly cooked, as in the following recipe, gai lan has an engaging crunchy texture that is almost addictive. Italian broccoli (rapini) is a fairly close substitute. Regular broccoli will work if you can't find either.

1 lb	gai lan or broccoli	500 g
3 cups	Chicken Stock (p. 3) or Vegetable Stock (p. 4)	750 mL
½ tsp	sugar	2 mL
2	slices ginger	2
1 tsp	sesame oil	5 mL
1 tbsp	oyster sauce	15 mL

1. Trim off woody bottoms of gai lan stems and cut any thick parts of stems in half lengthwise. Cut into 3-inch/8 cm pieces.
2. In wok, bring stock, sugar and ginger to boil over high heat. Add gai lan to stock and cook uncovered for about 2 minutes or until just tender.
3. Toss gai lan with sesame oil and oyster sauce. Arrange on platter and serve immediately.

Serves 4

Gai Lan
Chinese broccoli

Its dull, waxy green stems and leaves turn a most attractive deep green when cooked. Look for stems that are pencil-thick or slightly thicker and about 6 to 8 inches/15 to 20 cm long, with healthy looking bud clusters and white flowers at the top. White dots on the bottom indicate stems that are too mature and tough for good eating.

Each serving provides:

	Calories	48
g	Carbohydrates	5
g	Protein	3
g	Fat	3
g	Saturated Fat	tr
mg	Cholesterol	0
g	Fibre	2
mg	Sodium	187
mg	Potassium	265

Excellent: vitamin C
Good: folacin

Sauteed Mustard Greens with Garlic

Gai choy, *one of the oldest cultivated vegetables in China, is a taste treat. Apart from the usual uses when fresh, practically every culinary region in China has its own version of a gai choy pickle ranging from sweet and sour to savoury and chili-hot.*

1 lb	trimmed and cored mustard greens	500 g
1 tbsp	canola oil	15 mL
2	slices fresh ginger	2
1 tbsp	minced garlic	15 mL
½ cup	Rich Pork Stock (p. 8) or Chicken Stock (p. 3)	125 mL

1. Cut mustard greens across stems into 1-inch/2.5 cm pieces.
2. In wok, heat oil over high heat. Add ginger and mustard greens and stir until well coated with oil. Add garlic and stock and stir to mix.
3. Cover and steam for 2 minutes, stirring once or twice. Add leaf pieces and stir to mix. Cover and steam for 1 minute or until mustard greens are just tender.
4. Uncover and stir until almost all liquid in wok evaporates, about 1 minute. Discard ginger. Place mustard greens on platter and serve.

Serves 4

Gai Choy
Mustard greens

Gai choy, with its subtle mustard flavour, is one of many types of mustard greens. Mature bunches usually come with the large, fibrous leaves trimmed off. When braised, the stalks are wonderfully moist and tender. You can often find younger, smaller, leafier gai choy with thin, ribbed stalks and serrated leaves. It is milder and can be prepared the same way with less cooking or used in salads as you would romaine lettuce.

Each serving provides:

	Calories	65
g	Carbohydrates	7
g	Protein	3
g	Fat	4
g	Saturated Fat	tr
mg	Cholesterol	0
g	Fibre	2
mg	Sodium	29
mg	Potassium	422

Excellent: vitamin A; vitamin C; folacin
Good: vitamin E

Cubed Garlic Yams

Very often at the beginning of a Chinese meal some small snacks will be served to whet the appetite. This dish is not particularly traditional, but I like it for its sweet flavour. It reminds me of the roasted yams that I used to buy on the street in Hong Kong.

4	medium yams or sweet potatoes	4
4 tsp	soy sauce	20 mL
3 tbsp	Chinese-style Vegetable Stock (p. 5)	45 mL
3 tbsp	sugar	45 mL
1 tbsp	sesame oil	15 mL
3 tbsp	water	45 mL
1 tbsp	minced garlic	15 mL
¼ tsp	pepper	1 mL

1. Peel and cut yams into ½-inch/1 cm cubes, then rinse and drain well.
2. In medium saucepan combine soy sauce, stock, sugar, sesame oil, water and garlic, mixing well. Add yams and bring to boil.
3. Lower heat to medium. Cover and simmer for about 10 minutes or until yams are just becoming tender, stirring occasionally. If necessary, add water to prevent sauce from burning.
4. Uncover and bring to boil over high heat. Cook, stirring, until all liquid is absorbed and the yams are glazed, about 5 minutes. Season with grindings of black pepper. Serve warm or cold.

Serves 5

Each serving provides:

	Calories	245
g	Carbohydrates	53
g	Protein	4
g	Fat	3
g	Saturated Fat	tr
mg	Cholesterol	0
g	Fibre	6
mg	Sodium	293
mg	Potassium	648

Excellent: fibre; vitamin A; vitamin C

Good: riboflavin; vitamin B-6; folacin

114

Sesame Spinach

Simplicity never tasted so good. This spinach is a great side dish with any meal, especially if you are serving roast duck, barbecued items or broiled beef.

4 cups	water	1 L
2 lb	spinach leaves, washed and trimmed	1 kg
1 tbsp	sesame oil	15 mL
¼ tsp	salt	1 mL
1 tbsp	toasted sesame seeds	15 mL

1. Bring water to boil. Add spinach and blanch for 1 minute or until leaves are just wilted. Drain and rinse under cold water until spinach is thoroughly cooled. Drain well and squeeze spinach in clean, dry towel to remove excess moisture.
2. Place spinach in medium bowl and sprinkle on sesame oil and salt. Stir to mix well.
3. Sprinkle with sesame seeds for garnish and serve.

Serves 4

Each serving provides:

	Calories	93
g	Carbohydrates	9
g	Protein	7
g	Fat	5
g	Saturated Fat	1
mg	Cholesterol	0
g	Fibre	6
mg	Sodium	312
mg	Potassium	1276

Excellent: fibre; vitamin A; vitamin E; vitamin C; riboflavin; folacin; iron
Good: calcium

115

Oriental Mushroom Pickle

Serve these mushrooms as a pickle, in combination with the Cubed Garlic Yams or Sesame Spinach on the previous pages or as a trio of side vegetables for a large group of diners. Button mushrooms, which develop a meaty texture, work best in this recipe.

5 cups	button mushrooms, whole	1.25 L
1 tbsp	olive oil	15 mL
¼ cup	Vegetable Stock (p. 4) or Chinese-style Vegetable Stock (p. 5)	50 mL
¼ cup	white wine vinegar	50 mL
4 tsp	soy sauce	20 mL
¼ cup	minced garlic	50 mL
¼ cup	chopped green onion	50 mL

1. In medium saucepan, combine all ingredients except green onions and bring to boil.
2. Reduce heat to medium and cook about 15 minutes or until liquid is mostly absorbed. Stir occasionally.
3. Remove from heat and allow to cool. Add green onions, toss to mix and serve.

Serves 5

Each serving provides:

	Calories	59
g	Carbohydrates	7
g	Protein	3
g	Fat	3
g	Saturated Fat	tr
mg	Cholesterol	0
g	Fibre	1
mg	Sodium	313
mg	Potassium	322

Excellent: vitamin D

Good: riboflavin

Spicy Cucumber Salad

Here's a quick pickle that will add a bit of spice to a simple meal. Try it with Steamed Chicken Buns (p. 38) or Lamb and Leek Rolls (p. 98) for lunch, or use it as a garnish for a simple meat dish like Spicy Tangerine Beef (p. 93).

1 1/2 tsp	sugar	7 mL
1/2 tsp	salt	2 mL
1/2 tsp	hot red pepper flakes	2 mL
1 tsp	minced garlic	5 mL
1 tbsp	white wine vinegar	15 mL
1 tbsp	chopped green onion, optional	15 mL
1	English cucumber, thinly sliced	1
1 tbsp	toasted sesame seeds	15 mL

1. Combine sugar, salt, hot pepper flakes, garlic, vinegar and green onion and mix well.
2. Add sliced cucumber and toss until well coated. Let stand in refrigerator for 20 minutes.
3. Just before serving, sprinkle with sesame seeds.

Serves 5

Each serving provides:		
	Calories	24
g	Carbohydrates	4
g	Protein	1
g	Fat	1
g	Saturated Fat	0
mg	Cholesterol	0
g	Fibre	1
mg	Sodium	215
mg	Potassium	106

Sui Choy

Napa cabbage, Chinese cabbage, wong nga bak

This staple green of northern China is available almost everywhere. It is deliciously sweet when braised or cooked in soups. Because of its size and tightly packed leaves, this cabbage can be kept for up to two weeks in the refrigerator and makes a good pantry item. Just discard the dry, wilted leaves on the outside. Savoy cabbage is a good substitute.

Sui Choy with Cream Sauce

We've duplicated an indulgent banquet dish here. In the original recipe the cream sauce is flavoured with diced ham. We have removed the ham and replaced the cream with skim milk powder to good effect.

1½ lb	sui choy or savoy cabbage	750 g
1 cup	Rich Pork Stock (p. 8) or Chicken Stock (p. 3), divided	250 mL
3 tbsp	dry skim milk powder	45 mL
1 tbsp	cornstarch	15 mL
1 tbsp	canola oil	15 mL
¼ tsp	salt	1 mL
½ tsp	sugar	2 mL
½ tsp	Japanese seven-spice or white pepper	2 mL

1. Wash and cut leaves into 1½-inch/3.5 cm slices.
2. Combine milk powder and cornstarch with ¼ cup/50 mL of the stock and whisk until smooth. Set aside.
3. Heat oil in skillet or wok over medium heat. Add cabbage and stir-fry about 1 minute. Add salt, sugar and remainder of stock. Stir and bring to boil. Cover and cook for 3 minutes or until cabbage is tender.
4. Add cornstarch mixture and heat until sauce thickens. Sprinkle with Japanese seven-spice or white pepper and serve.

Serves 4

Vegetarian Eggplant Szechuan Style

The original recipe is flavoured with ground pork, but we have converted it to a vegan dish. If you are not vegan, try using Shrimp Stock (p. 6) for extra flavour.

| 2 | dried Chinese mushrooms, soaked and finely chopped | 2 |
| 4 | medium Chinese or Japanese eggplants | 4 |

Sauce:

1 tsp	soy sauce	5 mL
2 tsp	Chinese black vinegar or balsamic vinegar	10 mL
1 tsp	brown sugar	5 mL
1/2 tsp	sesame oil	2 mL
1/2 cup	Vegetable Stock (p. 4)	125 mL

Thickener:

| 2 tbsp | Vegetable Stock or Chinese-style Vegetable Stock (p. 5) | 25 mL |
| 2 tsp | cornstarch | 10 mL |

1 tbsp	canola oil	15 mL
1 tsp	minced garlic	5 mL
1 1/2 tsp	minced ginger	7 mL
2 tbsp	chopped onion	25 mL
2 tsp	hot bean paste	10 mL
1/2 cup	finely chopped fresh mushrooms	125 mL
2 tbsp	chopped green onion	25 mL

1. As mushrooms soak, remove stalks of eggplants and cut into thumb-sized pieces. Steam over high heat for 10 minutes. Remove and set aside.
2. Combine sauce mixture and set aside. Combine thickening mixture and set aside.
3. In non-stick skillet or wok, heat oil. Add garlic, ginger and onion and stir-fry for 15 seconds. Add hot bean paste and fresh and reconstituted mushrooms and cook for 1 minute. Add steamed eggplant and sauce mixture and bring to boil; continue to cook for 1 minute.
4. Add thickener and stir until sauce is thickened. Remove from heat, sprinkle with green onions, stir to mix and serve.

Serves 5

Chinese Eggplant
Japanese eggplant

This elongated cousin of the western eggplant generally sports a lighter purple skin. It has fewer seeds than the round eggplants and the peel is less bitter, so it doesn't need to be salted and sweated before cooking. It will not keep as long as the regular eggplant, so look for plump, firm ones and use them within 2 days.

Each serving provides:

	Calories	119
g	Carbohydrates	20
g	Protein	3
g	Fat	4
g	Saturated Fat	tr
mg	Cholesterol	0
g	Fibre	6
mg	Sodium	236
mg	Potassium	617

Excellent: fibre

Good: vitamin D; folacin

Sauteed Pea Sprouts and Oyster Mushrooms

Pea Sprouts

Pea sprouts are the young sprouts of the snow pea plant. If you can't find sprouts, pea tops, the snow pea shoots, are quite widely available. Both have a fresh, nutty flavour and cook quickly. Try them in salads too; they have a great snow pea flavour when raw. They do not store very well after rinsing, so buy and store them dry, then revitalize them in ice water just before cooking.

Sauce:

¾ cup	Rich Pork Stock (p. 8) or Chicken Stock (p. 3)	175 mL
2 tsp	cornstarch	10 mL
1 tbsp	fish sauce	15 mL
1 tbsp	canola oil	15 mL
½ lb	oyster mushrooms	250 g
1 tbsp	minced garlic	15 mL
¼ cup	Rich Pork Stock or Chicken Stock	50 mL
½ tsp	Japanese seven-spice or white pepper	2 mL
½ lb	pea sprouts or pea tops	250 g

1. Mix together sauce ingredients and set aside.
2. In wok, heat oil over medium-high heat. Add oyster mushrooms and garlic and saute for 2 minutes or until mushrooms are softened. Add a little water or stock to moisten mushrooms if necessary. Season with Japanese seven-spice. Remove mushrooms and keep warm.
3. Add sauce mixture to wok and bring to boil. Add pea sprouts and toss until well coated. Cook for about 1 minute or until sprouts are just wilted and sauce is slightly thickened.
4. Transfer sprouts to warm serving plate, top with mushrooms and serve immediately.

Serves 5

Each serving provides:

	Calories	175
g	Carbohydrates	27
g	Protein	11
g	Fat	4
g	Saturated Fat	tr
mg	Cholesterol	2
g	Fibre	4
mg	Sodium	303
mg	Potassium	202

Excellent: folacin

Good: fibre; iron

Eggplant Chickpea Sandwiches

I grew up enjoying the best of the East and West. My cooking is inspired by both, so I make no apologies for this "fusion" dish inspired by the cuisine of the Mediterranean.

2 tbsp	balsamic vinegar	25 mL
2 tsp	sugar	10 mL
2	regular eggplants, cut crosswise in ½-inch/1 cm slices	2
1 tbsp	olive oil	15 mL
1	19-oz/540 mL tin chickpeas, rinsed and drained	1
2 tsp	minced ginger	10 mL
¼ cup	chopped green onions	50 mL
2 tsp	minced garlic	10 mL
¼ tsp	salt	1 mL
3	medium tomatoes, peeled, seeded, pureed	3
2 tbsp	finely chopped cilantro	25 mL
¼ tsp	sugar	1 mL
¼ tsp	white pepper	1 mL

1. Combine vinegar and sugar and brush onto eggplant slices.
2. Heat non-stick skillet over high heat. Add olive oil and saute eggplant slices for about 2 minutes on each side. Remove from pan and set on paper towel to absorb oil and excess moisture.
3. In food processor, puree chickpeas to thick paste. Add a few drops of water if required.
4. Over high heat, cook ginger, green onions and garlic in 2 tbsp/25 mL water for about 1 minute. Add salt and stir to mix. Add chickpea puree, mash together well, and continue to cook until warmed through.
5. Spread 1 eggplant slice with thick layer of chickpea paste, then place another eggplant slice on top. Continue making "sandwiches" until all ingredients are used. Using sharp knife, cut each eggplant sandwich in half. Arrange on plate and keep warm.
6. Heat tomato puree in saucepan over low heat until just warm. Be careful not to boil—tomato sauce should taste like fresh tomatoes. Stir in cilantro and season with sugar and white pepper. Pour sauce around eggplant sandwiches and serve.

Serves 4

Chickpeas
Garbanzo beans

Another of the legume family—a great source of protein. Unlike protein sources such as meat, poultry and dairy products, legumes provide very little fat and saturated fat, no cholesterol, and lots of soluble fibre.

Each serving provides:

	Calories	251
g	Carbohydrates	49
g	Protein	10
g	Fat	6
g	Saturated Fat	1
mg	Cholesterol	0
g	Fibre	14
mg	Sodium	341
mg	Potassium	1122

Excellent: fibre; folacin

Good: iron; vitamin C; thiamine; vitamin B-6

Jicama Root
Sha got

This native of the American tropics has recently grown dramatically in popularity. Used by the Chinese mainly for its starch, which is much like cornstarch, jicama is now widely available in supermarkets and Chinese groceries. It has a crunchy texture, which it retains when cooked, and a refreshingly mild pearlike flavour. Peel the brown skin off before using.

Each serving provides:

	Calories	90
g	Carbohydrates	19
g	Protein	4
g	Fat	tr
g	Saturated Fat	tr
mg	Cholesterol	3
g	Fibre	5
mg	Sodium	394
mg	Potassium	280

Excellent: vitamin A; iron

Good: fibre; vitamin C; vitamin B-12

Chinese Coleslaw

If you have trouble getting jicama, try substituting grated cabbage in this refreshing version of coleslaw.

Dressing:

1 tbsp	sugar, or to taste	15 mL
1 tbsp	fish sauce	15 mL
3 tbsp	fresh lime juice	45 mL
1 tbsp	cider vinegar	15 mL
1 ½ tsp	dried onion flakes, optional	7 mL
1 ½ tsp	dried garlic flakes, optional	7 mL

Salad:

2 cups	jicama, cut in matchsticks, or grated cabbage	500 mL
1 cup	cucumber, cut in matchsticks	250 mL
1 cup	carrots, cut in matchsticks	250 mL
¼ cup	chopped fresh mint	50 mL
¼ cup	chopped cilantro	50 mL

1. Combine all dressing ingredients and set aside to blend flavours for 10 minutes.
2. In dry skillet, toast onion and garlic flakes over medium-low heat until just golden. Set aside.
3. In large bowl, toss all salad ingredients except garlic and onion flakes together with dressing.
4. Arrange salad on platter and sprinkle with garlic and onion flakes. Serve with grilled or roasted meats or as a side dish.

Serves 4

Water Spinach with Shrimp Sauce

If shrimp sauce is a bit strong for you, use a cube of red fermented bean curd as the flavouring for this. Just mash it with the sherry. Red miso makes a passable replacement as well. If you can't find shrimp sauce, use the same volume of anchovies or anchovy paste. And vice versa! I've used shrimp sauce to replace anchovies in a Caesar salad dressing.

Sauce:

2 tsp	cornstarch	10 mL
½ cup	Chinese-style Vegetable Stock (p. 5) or Chicken Stock (p. 3)	125 mL
1 lb	water spinach or regular spinach	500 g
1½ tsp	canola oil	7 mL
1½ tsp	minced garlic	7 mL
1 tbsp	minced ginger	15 mL
1½ tsp	shrimp sauce	7 mL
2 tbsp	sherry	25 mL

1. Combine sauce ingredients and set aside.
2. Wash and trim water spinach. Cut into 2-inch/5 cm lengths.
3. Heat oil in wok over high heat. Add garlic, ginger, shrimp sauce and sherry and stir for 30 seconds.
4. Add water spinach and stir-fry for 1 minute. Cover and cook for 2 minutes, stirring occasionally.
5. Uncover, add sauce mixture, stir to mix well and cook until sauce is thickened. Serve immediately.

Serves 4

Water Spinach
Ong choy

Although it is cooked and eaten the same way as spinach, this is actually a swamp vegetable, with pale green arrowlike leaves and long hollow stems. It is crunchier and more subtly flavoured than spinach, but regular spinach works well in its place.

Each serving provides:

	Calories	51
g	Carbohydrates	4
g	Protein	4
g	Fat	2
g	Saturated Fat	tr
mg	Cholesterol	3
g	Fibre	2
mg	Sodium	203
mg	Potassium	493

Excellent: vitamin A;
vitamin E; vitamin C;
folacin
Good: iron

Braised Daikon and Chayote

Both daikon and chayote become sweet when braised, and they're enriched by the dried shrimp and ham in this dish. Now that you know about mo qua and winter melon, try substituting them for the chayote. If not, broccoli is also great in this dish. Just add it during the last five minutes of cooking.

If you'd like to make a vegan version, substitute good-quality Chinese mushrooms for the shrimp and ham and add one tablespoon of red miso. Use a combination of vegetable stock and mushroom liquid as the stock.

To make this a one-pot dish, add cooked chicken, beef or pork to it. Cooked beans and legumes also make a great final addition. Add them about 5 minutes before the vegetables are done to combine flavours.

6-inch	piece daikon, peeled, split lengthwise, or turnip	15 cm
1	chayote, split, seeded, peeled, or zucchini	1
1	carrot, peeled	1

Thickener:

2 tsp	cornstarch	10 mL
2 tbsp	water	25 mL
1½ tsp	canola oil	7 mL
1 tbsp	minced ginger	15 mL
2 tsp	minced garlic	10 mL
1	shallot, finely chopped	1
1 tbsp	dried shrimp	15 mL
1½ tsp	chopped Chinese ham or prosciutto	7 mL
8	mushrooms, halved	8
1 cup	Rich Pork Stock (p. 8) or Shrimp Stock (p. 6)	250 mL
1 tbsp	soy sauce	15 mL
2	green onions, sliced	2

1. Cut daikon, chayote and carrot into ½-inch/1 cm chunks.
2. Combine thickener and set aside.
3. In non-stick wok or large skillet, heat oil over medium-high heat. Add ginger, garlic, shallot, dried shrimp, ham and mushrooms and stir until fragrant, about 1 minute. Add stock, soy sauce and vegetables and stir to mix. Cover and simmer for 15 to 20 minutes, stirring occasionally to ensure even cooking. Test to see if vegetables are tender. When the daikon is cooked it will turn translucent.
4. Stir in green onions. Add thickener and bring to boil. Serve when sauce is slightly thickened.

Serves 4

Each serving provides:		
	Calories	80
g	Carbohydrates	14
g	Protein	3
g	Fat	2
g	Saturated Fat	tr
mg	Cholesterol	3
g	Fibre	4
mg	Sodium	305
mg	Potassium	514

Excellent: vitamin A;
vitamin C
Good: fibre; folacin

125

Sauteed Brussels Sprouts

Apparently, this simple way of doing brussels sprouts is all the rage in fancy restaurants in San Francisco. It's another validation of the tried-and-true Chinese method of underscoring simple vegetable dishes with a hint of garlic. I've made it a bit more filling with the pressed tofu.

1 tbsp	soft margarine	15 mL
1 lb	brussels sprouts, thinly sliced	500 g
2	pieces pressed tofu, cut in matchsticks	2
2 tsp	minced garlic	15 mL
¾ cup	Chicken Stock (p. 3) or Rich Pork Stock (p. 8)	175 mL
½ tsp	salt	2 mL
	black pepper to taste	

1. Heat large non-stick skillet or wok over medium-high heat. Add margarine and heat until just foaming. Add brussels sprouts, tofu and garlic and stir to mix for 30 seconds.
2. Add stock and season with salt and pepper. Stir and bring to boil. Cover and cook for 2 minutes or until brussels sprouts are just wilted but still crunchy. Uncover and cook until liquid is mostly absorbed. Serve.

Serves 6

Each serving provides:

	Calories	104
g	Carbohydrates	8
g	Protein	9
g	Fat	5
g	Saturated Fat	1
mg	Cholesterol	0
g	Fibre	4
mg	Sodium	216
mg	Potassium	354

Excellent: vitamin C; folacin; iron

Good: fibre; vitamin E

Papaya and Red Date Soup

For dessert the Chinese like to have soups, from swallow's nest at fancy banquets to the basic red (adzuki) bean soup that's served in virtually every restaurant. Hot or chilled, they are believed to aid digestion. Fresh fruit, such as orange or melon, is served after these sweet concoctions as a final course. I think it's a refreshing change from chocolate pâté, although my wife disagrees.

12	slices ginger	12
6 cups	water	1.5 L
30	Chinese red dates, or 15 dried figs	30
½ cup	honey	125 mL
2	ripe papayas	2

1. In saucepan, combine first 4 ingredients, cover and bring to boil. Reduce heat and simmer covered for 1 hour or until dates are soft.
2. Meanwhile, slice papayas in half and remove seeds. With small melon baller, make as many papaya balls as possible (or cut into medium dice). Add remaining juice from papaya skins to simmering soup.
3. Remove saucepan from heat and remove ginger slices. For clearer soup, strain through cheesecloth-lined sieve and return red dates to soup. Add papaya balls. Serve soup hot or cold. Remember, the dates have pits!

Serves 8

Each serving provides:

	Calories	112
g	Carbohydrates	29
g	Protein	1
g	Fat	tr
g	Saturated Fat	tr
mg	Cholesterol	0
g	Fibre	2
mg	Sodium	4
mg	Potassium	271

Excellent: vitamin C

Fresh Mango Pudding

This simple dessert captures the glorious essence of mangoes like no other. Its texture is silky rich and its taste, simply wonderful. Fresh cream is called for in the original recipe, but evaporated milk gives it the same richness without the fat.

2	envelopes unflavoured gelatin	2
¾ cup	sugar	175 mL
1 cup	hot water	250 mL
3 cups	pureed fresh mangoes	750 mL
1 cup	2% evaporated milk	250 mL
8	ice cubes	8
	lime wedges, optional	
	fresh mango slices for garnish, optional	

1. Add gelatin and sugar to hot water and mix until dissolved and smooth.
2. In large bowl, mix mango puree, evaporated milk and ice cubes.
3. Pour gelatin mixture into mango mixture and stir until ice cubes are melted.
4. Pour mixture into jelly mould and chill until set, at least 3 hours.
5. To serve, dip jelly mould briefly in hot water then turn pudding out onto platter. Squeeze on some lime juice, garnish with mango slices if desired and serve. (Best eaten within a day.)

Serves 8

Each serving provides:

	Calories	208
g	Carbohydrates	49
g	Protein	5
g	Fat	1
g	Saturated Fat	tr
mg	Cholesterol	3
g	Fibre	4
mg	Sodium	42
mg	Potassium	345

Excellent: vitamin A; vitamin C

Good: fibre; vitamin E

Lychee Granita

See photo, page 92

This incredibly simple dessert was the star of one of our tasting sessions. The canned lychees are ready to use and have the same intensity of flavour as the fresh ones. Try the recipe with other exotic finds you may come across in your local ethnic markets, like jackfruit, and longans mangosteens. The vodka adds a bit of zip but is entirely optional.

2	19-oz/540 mL tins pitted lychees	2
3 tbsp	vodka, optional	45 mL
	lime juice to taste	
2	kiwi fruits, peeled and sliced, optional	2
4 to 6	strawberries	4 to 6

1. In blender or food processor, blend lychee and juice until liquefied.
2. Add vodka and mix well. Taste and adjust sweetness by adding lime juice.
3. Pour mixture into shallow glass or plastic pan, cover and place in freezer. Check after about 2 hours. When mixture is beginning to freeze, stir with fork so it doesn't freeze solid. Stir periodically until mixture freezes into consistency of sorbet. If using an ice-cream machine, follow manufacturer's instructions for sorbet.
4. About ½ hour before serving, remove lychee granita from freezer and allow to soften slightly in refrigerator or cool place. Mix well and serve in parfait bowls garnished with kiwi and strawberry slices.

Serves 4 or more

Mini Custard Tarts

You can use commercial frozen tart shells if you have to, but be aware that the fat content will be substantially higher in each serving. Our tart shell recipe contains 4 grams of fat, while the commercial ones can have 8 to 12 grams each.

Sweet Pastry:

1 lb	pastry flour	500 g
½ cup	sugar	125 g
pinch	salt	pinch
⅓ cup	baking powder	75 mL
½ lb	part-skim ricotta cheese	250 g
5 tbsp	skim milk	90 mL
2	egg whites	2
1 tbsp	vanilla extract	15 mL
¼ cup	diced butter	50 mL

1. Preheat oven to 350°F/180°C.
2. Blend first 5 ingredients in food processor. Add last 5 ingredients and pulse until dough forms sticky ball.
3. Roll pastry into thin sheet on floured surface. Cut into 24 5-inch/12 cm circles. Make tart shells in regular muffin tins. Prebake in centre of oven for 3 to 5 minutes or until shells are slightly golden. Add filling and bake as directed.

Filling:

6	eggs	6
1½ cups	evaporated skim milk	375 mL
1 cup	sugar	250 mL
1 tsp	vanilla extract	5 mL

1. Heat oven to 350°F/180°C.
2. Beat all filling ingredients together.
3. Carefully pour filling mixture into prebaked tart shells until about ⅔ full. Bake in centre of oven for about 20 minutes. Insert metal skewer into centre; if it comes out clean they are done. Serve warm or at room temperature.

Serves 24

Each serving provides:		
	Calories	178
g	Carbohydrates	30
g	Protein	6
g	Fat	4
g	Saturated Fat	2
mg	Cholesterol	61
g	Fibre	1
mg	Sodium	323
mg	Potassium	84

Good: riboflavin; calcium

Poached Pears and Figs

For this recipe, choose pears that are a bit underripe. You can use the round, brown Chinese pears, which have a crisp texture like apples, but if you do, reduce the cooking time and check frequently, as they cook faster than Bartlett pears.

4 cups	water, or enough to cover fruit	1 L
1	cinnamon stick	1
3	Bartlett pears, peeled, cored and halved	3
12	dried figs, washed and halved	12
12	Chinese almonds or 1 tsp/5 mL almond extract, optional	12
1/3 cup	honey, or to taste	75 mL
6	sprigs mint for garnish	6

1. In non-aluminum saucepan, combine all ingredients and bring to boil.
2. Reduce heat to low and simmer for 30 to 45 minutes or until pears are tender when tested with a fork.
3. Adjust sweetness to taste by adding honey. Transfer to serving bowls, garnish with mint sprigs and serve hot or chilled.

Serves 6

Each serving provides:

	Calories	223
g	Carbohydrates	57
g	Protein	2
g	Fat	1
g	Saturated Fat	tr
mg	Cholesterol	0
g	Fibre	5
mg	Sodium	5
mg	Potassium	353

Good: fibre; vitamin E

Stewed Fruit and Kumquats with Dessert Tofu

Dessert tofu is a lighter form of tofu that is very soft and contains a lot more water. Fresh warm dessert tofu ladled out of a wooden bucket and sweetened with simple syrup is still one of my fondest childhood food memories. In supermarkets, dessert tofu comes in the same kind of packages as medium and soft tofu. Two types are available: sweetened and almond flavoured. If you don't fancy dessert tofu, serve this compote with non-fat vanilla yogurt.

1 cup	prunes, tightly packed, rinsed	250 mL
1 cup	dried apricots, tightly packed, rinsed	250 mL
2 cups	water	500 mL
4	pieces candied ginger, sliced	4
6	kumquats, thinly sliced, or 2 tbsp/25 ml candied orange peel	6
½ cup	orange juice	125 mL
2–3 tbsp	honey, to taste	25–45 mL
1½ lb	dessert tofu	750 g

1. Soak prunes and apricots in water overnight.
2. Transfer fruit mixture to non-aluminum saucepan with water, add ginger and bring to boil over medium heat. Simmer for 10 minutes or until fruit is plump and tender, stirring to ensure even cooking. Remove from heat and allow to cool.
3. Remove fruit from liquid, drain and remove prune pits. Reserve poaching liquid in saucepan.
4. Add orange juice and honey to poaching liquid and bring to boil.
5. Reduce heat to low, add sliced kumquats and simmer for 5 minutes or until tender. Remove from heat, add poached fruit and gently stir. Taste for sweetness and adjust with more honey if desired—the mixture should be quite sweet as it will be diluted by the tofu.
6. Drain tofu of excess water and transfer gently into large bowl or individual bowls.
7. To serve the dish warm, warm tofu in microwave oven or in steamer for 3 minutes, pour fruit compote over tofu and serve. To serve cold, or if you wish to prepare it ahead, refrigerate fruit compote overnight, then serve with tofu.

Serves 4

Each serving provides:		
	Calories	361
g	Carbohydrates	84
g	Protein	6
g	Fat	2
g	Saturated Fat	tr
mg	Cholesterol	0
g	Fibre	7
mg	Sodium	47
mg	Potassium	849

Excellent: fibre; vitamin A; vitamin E; vitamin C; iron

Good: thiamine; vitamin B-6; folacin

133

Gingered Mandarin Custard

This oriental version of crème caramel is lighter because we used more egg whites than egg yolks. The mandarin oranges and ginger give it a unique twist. Serve it with drained non-fat yogurt if you have a yen for the whipped cream that generally comes with crème caramel. This dessert provides more calcium than an 8-ounce glass of milk.

Mandarin Caramel:

1	7 1/2-oz/213 mL tin mandarin oranges	1
1/3 cup	sugar	75 mL

Custard:

4 cups	evaporated skim milk	1 L
6	slices ginger, smashed	6
1 tsp	vanilla extract	5 mL
4	large eggs	4
8	egg whites	8
1 cup	sugar	250 mL

1. Preheat oven to 300°F/150°C.
2. In food processor or blender, puree mandarin oranges and liquid until liquefied. Strain juice to get rid of pulp.
3. In small saucepan, boil sugar and mandarin juice until liquid begins to caramelize and reaches consistency of thick syrup. Divide and pour mandarin syrup into 8 heatproof bowls. Cool thoroughly.
4. In medium saucepan, combine milk, ginger slices and vanilla and bring almost to boiling point over medium heat. Remove from heat and let sit for 10 minutes. Strain and discard ginger slices.
5. Meanwhile, combine eggs, egg whites and sugar and beat until sugar is dissolved.
6. Finish custard by pouring milk in steady stream into egg mixture while stirring to mix. Skim off surface bubbles. Pour custard gently over syrup in bowls. Place bowls in deep baking pan. Pour enough hot water into tray to come halfway up sides of bowls. Cover tray with foil and bake for 1 to 1 1/4 hours or until a metal skewer inserted in custard comes out clean.
7. Remove custards from tray and refrigerate overnight or until chilled.
8. To serve, cut around edge of custard in bowl. Invert serving plate over bowl and quickly turn both over. Gently unmould custard, garnish with mandarin slices if desired and serve.

Serves 8

Each serving provides:

	Calories	295
g	Carbohydrates	52
g	Protein	16
g	Fat	3
g	Saturated Fat	1
mg	Cholesterol	111
g	Fibre	tr
mg	Sodium	235
mg	Potassium	549

Excellent: calcium: vitamin
D: riboflavin: vitamin B-12
Good: zinc

Index